I'LL QUIT TOMORROW

I'LL QUIT TOMORROW

Vernon E. Johnson

HARPER & ROW, PUBLISHERS
New York, Hagerstown, San Francisco, London

 For information address Harper & Row, Publishers, Inc., 10 East 53rd Street, New York, N.Y. 10022. Published simultaneously in Canada by Fitzhenry & Whiteside Limited, Toronto.

Library of Congress Cataloging in Publication Data

Johnson, Vernon E
I'll quit tomorrow.

1. Alcoholism. 2. Alcoholism—Treatment.
3. Alcoholics—Rehabilitation. I. Title.
[DNLM: 1. Alcoholism—Popular works. WM274 J69i
1973]
HV5035.J64 616.8'51 72-11356
ISBN 0-06-064172-X

Designed by C. Linda Dingler

77 78 20 19 18 17 16 15 14

Contents

Acknowledgments

Mark Twain is reported to have originated the observation "Adam had all the best of it. When *he* said something he *knew* no one had ever said it before!" One has to wonder if Twain really thought of *that* first. In any case, it is an apt phrase to describe the quandary of this writer in making acknowledgments regarding sources and resources for the thoughts on the following pages. No claim to originality can be made. Nor is it made. One only wishes one could remember each source. Proper credit would gladly and gratefully be made.

From unnumbered sick individuals, Alcoholics Anonymous members, physicians, clergymen, other professionals, has come information and insight. This effort has been simply to synthesize and give order to their contributions.

Three special groups must be given my thanks: first, the hospitals, their patients, their forward-looking boards, and administrative and medical staffs (pioneers in spirit, every one of them); second, the people at Hazelden, Center City, Minnesota, under the guidance of Dr. Dan Anderson, and third, those of the board of the Institute itself. "May they live long on the land and prosper!"

Over the years, associates in the work have been many—over fifty, in fact. If mentioned by name surely I will overlook some. I know they will understand if I say to them simply, "Thank you. I feel much more like I do now than I did when we started!"

Nevertheless, individual thanks must go to Barbara Heines, secretary, confidante, and friend, whose struggles through hen scratches brought it all to the publisher.

Finally, there is Mary Ann, whose long suffering permitted absences frequently, tardiness often, and whose compassion still answers the constantly jangling home telephone with patience with patients. This book is dedicated to the most "normal" person I know—my wife.

Introduction

Alcoholism is a fatal disease, 100 percent fatal. Nobody survives alcoholism that remains unchecked. We would estimate that 10 percent of the drinkers in America will become alcoholic, and that these people will not be able to stop drinking by themselves. It is a myth that alcoholics have some spontaneous insight and then seek treatment. Victims of this disease do not submit to treatment out of spontaneous insight—typically, in our experience they come to their recognition scenes through a buildup of crises that crash through their almost impenetrable defense systems. They are forced to seek help; and when they don't, they perish miserably.

This disease involves the whole man: physically, mentally, psychologically, and spiritually. The most significant characteristics of the disease are that it is primary, progressive, chronic, and fatal. But it can be arrested. The progress of alcoholism can be stopped, and the patient can be recovered. Not cured, but recovered. This is a hardheaded, pragmatic statement of fact which has visible proof in the recovery of thousands of alcoholics who are well today. They are alive, and they bring alive hope for countless others. Their return gives the lie to the notion that this illness is too complex and too individual by nature even to tackle.

At the Johnson Institute in Minneapolis, Minnesota, we have had the privilege of assisting in the development of three such treatment programs in private general hospitals in Minnesota and Nebraska. The oldest is in its fifth year in St. Mary's Hospital in Minneapolis, where a 52-bed unit is available for treatment of this disease. The programs in these three hospitals have recovered thousands who were desperately sick. These people have returned to happy and productive lives—not the bleak, unrewarding, abstinent existence that is associated with arrested alcoholism.

Very simply, the treatment involves a therapy designed to bring the patient back to reality. The course of treatment consists of an average of four weeks of intensive inpatient care of the acute symptoms in the hospital, and up to two years of aftercare as an outpatient.

Annual studies of St. Mary's former patients have consistently indicated that 52 percent of the patients never drink again after completing the program. The other 48 percent relapse and experiment with alcohol. About half of these dropouts return and complete the outpatient program successfully, and remain abstinent. This means that in the end three out of four of St. Mary's patients successfully recover from alcoholism. Continuing studies of the patients at the other two hospitals have indicated almost exactly parallel results.

The myths and old wives' tales around alcoholism are legion. When you demythologize it, you find that this disease is an entity as distinct as measles. Alcoholism has a describable, predictable pattern of pathology. It is primary in the sense that it effectively blocks any care or treatment we might want to deliver to any other problem; if an alcoholic has a diseased liver, which he frequently does, the doctor cannot do anything about the liver until the alcoholism is brought under control. Our observation of the illness leads us to believe that it is always progressive. It never plateaus. It always worsens.*

Who contracts this illness? What sort of personality becomes alcoholic? The answer seems to be that, mysteriously, all sorts of personalities become alcoholic. The fact is that the cause of alcoholism is unknown. The difficult question, in fact, is why some people cannot become alcoholic no matter how hard they try. A drinker has to be able to develop a tolerance for ethyl alcohol or he can't make it. If alcohol makes him sick and he throws up, he is immune. Drinking is not enough—you have to get drunk to become alcoholic, but even the definition of drunkenness can cause endless debate.

Our most startling observation has been that alcoholism cannot exist unless there is a conflict between the values and the behavior of the drinker.

People of every stripe of character and morality become alcoholics, but ultimately the disease causes all its victims to behave in a destructive and antisocial way. In searching for common denominators, we have observed that the alcoholic is likely to be an achiever in his peer group. Interestingly, people who appear entirely phlegmatic seem less likely to become addicted to alcohol or other mood-changing chemi-

*We mention on p. 84 a plateau which may occur during recovery. This never happens in the illness itself.

cals. They just live along, and the frustrations of life don't seem to get to them—neither does alcohol. Another way of avoiding this conflict is not to care. Sociopaths appear to lack the values or conscience essential to the conflict we observe in alcoholics. They *actually* feel no guilt or shame.

Since it is not known why people become alcoholic, the Johnson Institute began to inquire into other areas. Why do people who have the disease wait so long to get treatment? Why do they suffer so long? To accept the necessity of such extreme suffering and such damage seemed unconscionable. Since alcoholism is progressive and fatal, it was evident that the most urgent need was to stop the process of the disease as early as possible. We were very much concerned about the popular conviction that you could not do anything with an alcoholic until he hit some ultimate bottom. A first effort of the Institute was to study 200 recovered alcoholics. Our questions were designed to find out why they suffered so long and what kept them from getting help. Our goal was to discover how they came to treatment.

Well, it turned out that we were asking the wrong questions in the wrong way. We repeatedly got reports from recovered alcoholics that they had simply seen the light, that a spontaneous insight had brought them to treatment. By redesigning the questions we came up with the information—and the truth: all these people had suffered a buildup of crises that brought them to a recognition of their condition. The crises themselves were usually fortuitously grouped together so that they broke through the almost impenetrable defenses of the victims of the disease, which were organized into highly efficient "denial systems."

It became clear to us that it was not only pointless but dangerous to wait until the alcoholic hit bottom. The crises everybody was trying to help him avoid could actually be employed to break through his defenses, by an act of intervention that could stop the downward spiral toward death. We came to understand that crises could be used creatively to bring about intervention. Because, in fact, in all the lives we studied it was only through crisis that intervention had occurred. This led to experimentation with useful methods of employing crisis at earlier stages of the disease.

For ten years now, people have charged the Institute with inventing a system of treatment based on creating crises. And our response is that we do not invent crisis, that it is not necessary to invent it. Every alcoholic is already surrounded by crises, no one of which is being used. All we have to do is to make those around him knowledgeable enough so that they can start using the crises. This makes it possible for them to move sooner, and to limit the very real damage to themselves that comes from living with a worsening situation. In a later chapter we will explain how crises can be employed to set up confrontations which can lead to successful treatment.

A misconception about alcoholism causes people to be fearful to confront alcoholics. We are told that the alcoholism may be a cover for some more serious emotional disorder, and that alcoholics can be shattered if they are cornered. Another misconception is that since he behaves the way he does, the alcoholic is heedless and does not care what damage his behavior causes. This leads to the erroneous assumption that he will be unresponsive to any attempts to help him. Because of his wide mood swings, the alcoholic is a formidable person to confront, and it is true that he is able skillfully to rationalize his own behavior. But in this book we will share our observations that the alcoholic does not smash so easily, and that there is an explanation for his careless behavior. Actually he is loaded with self-hatred which is repressed and unconscious, and he projects this onto the persons around him.

The people around an alcoholic do not realize how little he knows of himself and of his own behavior. He is *not* confronted by his own actions; many of them he is not even aware of, although those around him assume that he is. They believe that he sees himself as they see him. In point of fact, as the disease runs its course, he is increasingly deluded. He lives with increasing impairment of his judgment, and eventually loses touch with his emotions entirely. He has conscious and unconscious ways of forgetting painful experiences. It is a matter of self-survival. If a person is alcoholic, by definition he is unable to recognize the fact. Any attempt to interrupt his drinking or change his life-style he views as meddling.

Since the alcoholic is not going to have any spontaneous insight, and since his disease makes it so difficult to approach him, it is crucial that the persons close to him understand the nature of his problem. For they must take the initiative if the illness is to be arrested. One of the chief goals of this book is to explain why this is so and how to do it.

Very different sorts of people become alcoholic, but all alcoholics are ultimately alike. The disease itself swallows up all differences and creates a *universal alcoholic profile.* The personality changes that go with the illness are predictable and inevitable, with of course some individual adaptation. When we describe the behavior of a victim of this disease, there is always instant recognition by members of the family. The classic description fits almost any individual alcoholic to a startling degree.

It is our observation that the symptoms we find are present in victims addicted to other chemicals. In observing the effects of alcohol we have inevitably been forced to evaluate the effects of mood-changing chemicals such as the amphetamines, the barbiturates, and the minor tranquilizers. Persons dependent on these chemicals go through the same disintegration as the alcoholic. And they can be recovered by the same treatment that is proving so successful with alcoholics. Nowadays, a majority of alcoholics are simultaneously involved with other mood-changing chemicals. Our treatment was developed in the light of this reality, and is effective with multiple-chemical use.

The experimental programs in the field of alcoholism that led to the founding of the Johnson Institute began in 1962. The early studies were conducted within the framework of the parish of St. Martin's-by-the-Lake, an Episcopal church in Minneapolis which volunteered itself as a working laboratory. A four-man staff of clergymen devoted themselves to solving certain major problems in the community, one of which was alcoholism. Community leaders who saw the value of continuing work in this field then organized the Johnson Institute in 1966 as a non-profit foundation. Two basic goals were set up: to design specific programs for alcoholics through applied research, and to educate the public in methods of intervention. In pursuing these goals the foundation discovered that it was necessary to use a multidiscipline approach which would include the fields of medicine, psychology, sociology, theology, and practical drug experience.

We soon realized that we could not have an effective working laboratory unless we were directly involved in treating alcoholics. And treating alcoholics led us to the obvious conclusion that alcoholics should be treated where other sick people were treated—that is, in our general hospitals. So we were very fortunate when St. Mary's General Hospital approached us in 1966 about opening its doors to these patients. We started with 16 beds in a 600-bed hospital. They filled immediately, and we had a waiting list. The unit at St. Mary's grew from 16 to 25 beds, then 36, then 42, and eventually to 52 beds, or a full floor in the modern section of the hospital. From the first we designed the unit as simply another service for the medical staff. The admitting physician in this design is the attending physician. Some 200 doctors have used the service for their patients. The result has been the creation of a great medical resource for alcoholics.

Since the opening of the alcoholic unit at St. Mary's, our Institute has started programs in other hospitals, among the first of which were Miller Dwan General Hospital in Duluth, Minnesota, and Lincoln General Hospital in Lincoln, Nebraska. We are getting reinforcing statistics from these hospitals. This total experience supports our conviction that alcoholism can be effectively treated and that a large majority of alcoholics can be saved from an ignominious death.

In the next chapters we will describe our observations of the process by which the social drinker develops a chemical dependency and becomes alcoholic. This mood-changing drug can precipitate the onset of a disease with a predictable, inexorable course. It can ultimately destroy the physical, emotional, spiritual, and mental life of the victim. The disease is typified by a progressive "mental mismanagement" and an increasing emotional distress which can reach suicidal proportions. There is a developing spiritual impoverishment that makes the destruction complete. Because this pattern can now be specifically described, a specific form of treatment can be employed with predictable and significant recovery rates.

People who get sick with this disease can and do get well.

I.

A Drinking Culture

Let me get you a little dividend

As we begin to deal in detail with the progressive emotional distress of alcoholism, the fact that we can now be specific is worth noting. There has been very little precise information on the course of the disease. Virtually all of us in our society have been exposed to alcoholism in some form or other, and it has caused us great consternation and confusion. We have had no handle or method for approaching it which was specific enough so that we could take directions and set goals. Alcoholism has been as a health problem both too complex and too idiosyncratic to handle within the framework of conventional medical care.

Our approach at the Institute has been strictly pragmatic. We have not been out to prove any theory. We were simply given the opportunity to observe literally thousands of alcoholics, their families, and the other people surrounding them. All our trained and experienced personnel shared their observations, and we came up with the discovery that alcoholics showed certain specific conditions with a remarkable consistency. Such applied research then led to the development of experimental programs designed to try to meet these conditions and cope with them. As the years passed, we continued to use and refine the programs that worked in practice. A decade of such efforts is reported in this book.

First we noted that physical addiction with its withdrawal problems could be quite safely handled in a qualified medical setting. The process of detoxification is essentially the substitution of some other chemical for alcohol while the toxic effects of the alcohol subside. This process is generally completed within a few days. We can take care of the physical addiction with relative ease; the burden of the harmful dependency is psychological. Breaking through the psychological addiction is a much more complex and difficult problem.

Nevertheless, our continuing experience with increasing numbers of cases suggested that this condition could be accurately described in terms of a special kind of emotional distress found to be present in all of them. In order to illustrate this universal emotional pattern of alcoholism we used the Feeling Chart. This is essentially a straight-line graph where all human emotions can be represented. The mood swings which are the emotional symptoms of alcoholism are shown on successive graphs as we trace the inevitable deterioration of the self-image of the suffering alcoholic.

In Figure I below, human feelings are registered graphically from left to right. The most painful feelings at the far left merge into less painful ones, which shade into normal feelings and ultimately build to ecstatic emotions or the euphoria depicted at the far right of the graph. Thus the feelings range from suicidal despair to ecstasy. Theoretically, everybody is somewhere on this graph at any given moment. Since we all have mood swings, in a lifetime any of us would move over a large part of this spectrum. According to the law of averages, most of us would occupy the center of the graph during most of the days and years of our lives.

We have arbitrarily divided all human emotion into three feeling areas. We are not suggesting that the population is divided in this way. We do not know exactly how many human beings would fall into each category. But for the purpose of illustrating the dynamics of alcoholism or mood swings, the chart can be useful to us as a tool. Moods range from "I'm no damn good" up through "I'm okay," to "I'm blissful." We can assume that the great majority of persons are emotionally more or less comfortable and therefore in the middle of the chart. A significant fraction of the population live in chronic emotional pain and need help. While there are fewer profoundly or ecstatically happy people, at any one time they do exist. The question of how many there are in each category is not important. Inexplicably, alcoholism seems to hit approximately 10 percent of each of these groups as we roughly define them in considering our patients' earlier histories—the desolate and the joyful alike. One might think that people in chronic emotional pain would become alcoholic in disproportionate numbers, and on the other hand, that productive, well-adjusted individuals with integrated personalities would have a powerful immunity. On the basis of the thousands of alcoholics we have observed, this is not true of the conditions that precede their active alcoholism.

Joe loses his wife, becomes distraught with grief and starts drinking heavily. He does become helplessly alcoholic as a result. But Harry and Tom, who are also inconsolable with grief and who also try to drown their sorrows, do not become alcoholic. Since we cannot anticipate who will take the downward, disastrous path, the only productive way to study the disease is to consider thousands who already have a harmful dependency and retrace their progress into alcoholism. Before the onset of the disease, their emotional backgrounds are different. After they have contracted the illness, however, it becomes more and more apparent that the pattern of emotional distress is universal, and that chemically dependent people not only show the same pathology, but respond to the same treatment. We use the Feeling Chart to record the drinking experience of the alcoholic from the first phase, or introduction to ethyl alcohol, to the first instance of *emotional cost* which signals the onset of the disease, and finally to the last, fatal stage which may be either slow or rapid suicide.

The first two phases on the Feeling Chart, discovering or learning the mood swing and seeking the mood swing, are entirely pleasant and benign. They describe the experiences of all drinkers, not just alcoholics. The individual is introduced to some beverage containing ethyl alcohol (wine, beer, or distilled spirits), and in our culture this will likely be very early in life. It may be beer or liquor from the parents' supply. It may or may not taste good, but it is a significant discovery as a new feeling, and in no time most young drinkers get accustomed to the taste. In terms of the Feeling Chart, that first drinking experience is a mood swinger in a postive direction—it gives the drinker a warm, good feeling, may even make him giddy, depending upon the amount. And when the effects of the alcohol wear off, the drinker returns to normal (see Figure II). There is no damage, there is no emotional cost. On the chart he goes from 1 to 2, then swings back to 1 again when the effect disappears.

Figure II

PHASE ONE: LEARNS MOOD SWING

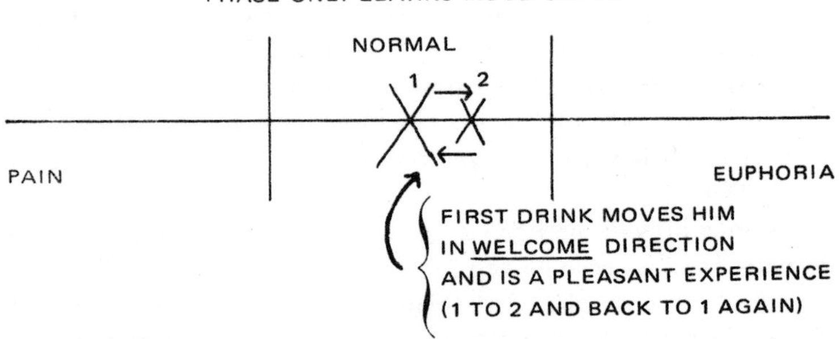

The initiation has been interesting and pleasant, and the only aftereffect is the exhilaration of a new experience. The new drinker is onto a good thing. The fact that he can make himself feel better is a real discovery. He can turn it on and he can turn it off. There are three steps in this learning experience. Alcohol always moves him in the right direction. He can control the degree of the mood swing by the amount. And it works every time. If one drink will do this, two or three will do *that.* It does not take very long to learn that he can set the amount and select the mood. He swings up into a relaxing mood, then swings back to home base. So, on the chart, it is 1 to 3 and then back to 1 again (see Figure III).

Notice, too, *how* he is learning. It is not from a lecture or a printed page—that is, didactically or intellectually. He is learning experientially, by doing it. And he is learning by feeling it, or emotionally, which is the very best way to absorb anything. This is the difference between learning to drive a car from behind the wheel—with the surge of power under your foot as you depress the accelerator and the landscape whipping by until you brake and grind to a stop—and a purely classroom type of experience with a good book on *How to Drive an Automobile.* There is no comparison between these learning processes.

Figure III

PHASE ONE: LEARNS MOOD SWING

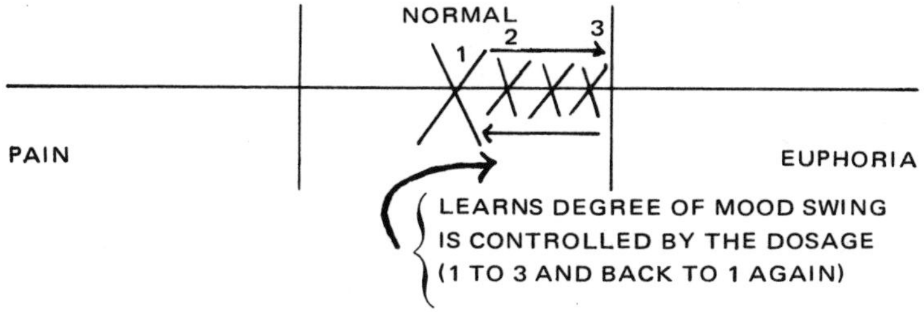

NORMAL

1 2 3

PAIN

EUPHORIA

LEARNS DEGREE OF MOOD SWING IS CONTROLLED BY THE DOSAGE (1 TO 3 AND BACK TO 1 AGAIN)

As the drinking continues, the learning process continues, and a lot of it is unconscious learning. But if it is subtle, it is thorough. He learns that alcohol *works every time.* So he is not only into the use of alcohol; he developes a relationship with it. This whole experience is absorbed, and in due time he knows that when he comes home and feels like *this,* with one drink he can feel like *that.* Or if it isn't enough and he wants to feel more like *that,* one or two more will do the trick. This relationship with alcohol is positive rather than negative. It is based on implicit trust, built in more and more strongly as experience proves that booze will do its job for him every time. Experience builds on experience and consolidates it, and the result is a deeply imbedded relationship *which he will carry through the rest of his life.*

No trouble yet! Quite the opposite. So now our happy social drinker moves into the second phase of his relationship with alcohol. He has learned that it works, that it is a positive experience, and that he can trust it—now he seeks mood swings in more or less regular and appropriate ways. In effect, he enters our drinking culture. And make no mistake, it *is* a drinking culture. Anybody who can become an alcoholic in America, will.

The cocktail hour is one of the primary American institutions. It is called the social hour by groups still timid about flaunting it. Alcohol is an integral part of all evening entertainment, unless there is some exceptional, special prohibition. Booze is an expected part of the entertainment of clients and customers, and it would take a bold business host to exclude it. This powerful chemical is moving down slowly to younger and younger age groups. Its appropriateness is decided on the basis of legal age. And even this consideration is frequently brushed aside. Alcohol has long since infiltrated the home, where it is styled as the ubiquitous "drink before dinner." Commercial airlines compete not only as to the comfort of their seats, but also in the frequency and quality of their alcoholic beverages.

How long our composite incipient alcoholic will remain in the confines of the social drinking scene is unpredictable. Just as it is impossible to predict who will become alcoholic, there is no way of telling how rapidly the process will move. He may pass in one side of social drinking and out the other in a relatively short time, or it may take years. If he is average, he will be a good old social drinker for a long, long time. There will be happy times, as he experiences them and recalls them later. Looking back, he may say wistfully, "I had a lot of fun drinking in those days. It was only in the last two years that all the trouble happened." Of course, he invariably overestimates the period of happy drinking and underestimates the bad years.

In the good times, he could even get drunk and it wasn't really a problem. There were a lot of celebrational occasions when he tied one on, and the only penalty was a hangover the next day—a price he was generally willing to pay. There was the day of the big raise. He rushed home elated, barely able to contain himself. "Honey, it happened! I got the raise and the promotion!" he bubbled over to his wife. "Get dressed—we're going to paint the town red tonight!" She did, and they did. And he did feel awful the next day. His head was throbbing, his stomach was in terrible shape. He felt as if he had been stuffed with cotton, and he was dying of thirst. But there was no remorse.

The way he responded to getting drunk is an important insight into the whole problem of alcoholism. A physical price was exacted, and he was able to pay it. From a bed of pain he could look back on the night before and say, "What a helluva night we had! Whooeeee—Great Stuff." The point is that he could react to the experience in such a way that he paid no emotional price for the misadventure. If his true emotions could have spoken, they would have said, "It was a big deal. It was a cause for celebrating, and we celebrated. Great fun while it lasted. Of course, I wouldn't do it again tonight, but it was worth it."

The dialogue is unspoken. It has not been a mental but an emotional reaction. He was not *thinking* these things, he was *feeling* them. The big blast appears on the next Feeling Chart in the form of a big mood swing to euphoria, and then a backswing—but stopping at normal.

It was a real swing to 4, and he did gain plenty of momentum on the backswing. Physically he felt bad, but psychologically it was a safe return right back to the starting point. It was like swinging out over

Figure IV

PHASE TWO: SEEKS MOOD SWING

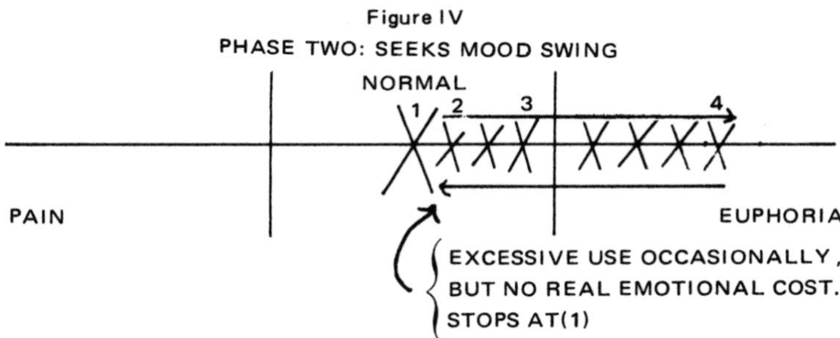

a hillside on a rope, and riding it back in to the starting point. This is Phase Two in the drinking experience—he contracts for the mood swings and makes them safely. But if he is going to become alcoholic, the terms of his experience with alcohol will begin to change.

As our social drinker gets deeper into his chemical, getting drunk begins to have a very different effect on him, and he is caught in an undertow which inexorably carries him out beyond social drinking. He is completely unaware that he is beyond his depth. He thinks things are going along swimmingly. But mysteriously, he has passed an invisible line that he cannot get back across by himself. He has entered Phase Three, which is alcoholism, by becoming *harmfully* dependent. *Why,* we can't say. But *how* is thoroughly describable, both behaviorally and emotionally. The index of the progress of the disease is the degree of the emotional cost. Graphically, the emotional price paid is recorded on the Feeling Chart below in terms of the mood swing back beyond normal toward pain.

Figure V

PHASE THREE: HARMFUL DEPENDENCE

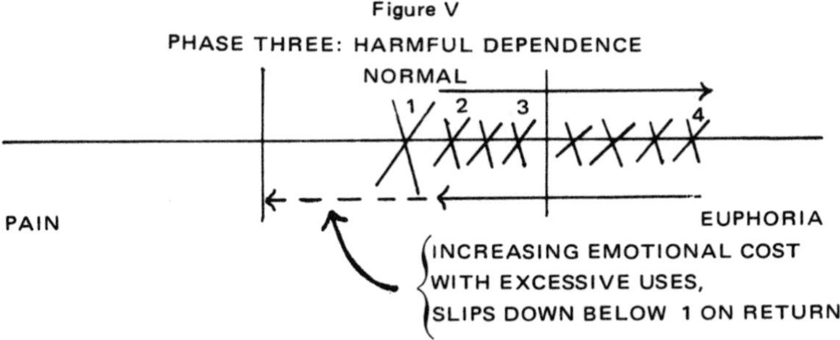

2.

The Rising Cost of Dependency

"Booze never affected me like this before"

The third phase of alcoholism opens with the onset of the disease in a recognizable form. We can describe it, it has its symptoms, and it has an inevitable course. This phase is characterized by harmful dependency and a rising emotional cost. We will see a significant and progressive deterioration of the personality of the alcoholic, and eventually a visible physical deterioration. Violent events begin to take place in the psyche of the alcoholic. Ultimately his whole emotional environment is riven and destroyed.

Remember, he is getting drunk and now paying a progressive emotional cost (see Figure VI) every time. The carefree days are gone, but he is only dimly aware of this. The fact that he will pay that rising price, and in order to make the payments actually recycle his personality, is definite proof that his dependency on the chemical has become truly harmful. This evidence of dependency will be progressively

Figure VI
PHASE THREE: HARMFUL DEPENDENCE

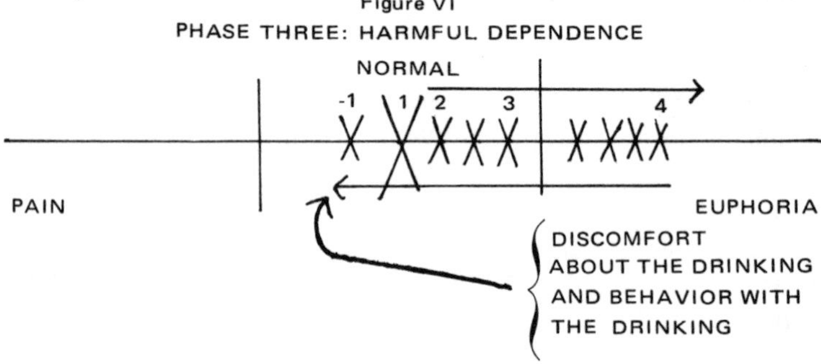

reinforced, as the alcoholic fails to comprehend the increasingly clear signs that booze is destroying him. As this happens, he is spending emotional capital and is unconsciously paying out an increasingly impossible amount of blackmail to his compulsion. This gradually becomes more than he can tolerate. There is a fateful, unconscious shift inside the alcoholic.

Emotionally, he is overwhelmed somewhere in that terrifying backswing of mood, and intellectual defenses rise in him against the emotional punishment. This is entirely unconscious. Drinking has become uncomfortable for him. He can no longer successfully pretend that it was worth it. Against this onslaught, automatically and invariably the intellectual defenses rise. He will instinctively, and with no particular notice of what he is doing, rationalize his feelings of discomfort about self. "I know why that happened," he will say about some particularly unyielding experience. "I did that on an empty stomach. Nobody can drink three martinis in an hour on an empty stomach."

What might appear to be a simple and harmless excuse to the self is more than that: this intellectual defense is actually the beginning of a relentless suppression of the emotions by the intellect. The alcoholic is learning to live his life more and more intellectually. His intellect will blindly defend against reason, against intervention, and will protect his disintegration right up to the ultimate brink. Eventually, ironically, he will be out of touch with his own emotions—he will not even know how he feels.

His little dialogues with himself will become the audio of an increasingly impenetrable defense system. After another bad evening, he will tell himself that the fool host delayed dinner until 11:30. "He was bombing us. They filled your glass before it was empty. Good thing I took care of my wife's drinks or they would have killed her. Yeah. Next time I'll drink a glass of milk or have a snack before I go to *that* house for dinner." And of course next time he won't drink so much, either; he is planning what he is going to do when he doesn't.

Unfortunately for him, the rationalization works. He feels better about himself. The tragedy is that he will continue to employ this form of defense as the illness progresses. Indeed, as time goes on, his behavior will become increasingly bizarre, and his innate ability to rationalize will be practiced to the point of perfection. This development will take place gradually, invisibly to himself, insidiously and imperceptibly, and with disastrous results.

Don't forget, *all* people instinctively rationalize when they are confronted with feelings of failure, and this includes entirely normal people who are in consistent fashion relatively comfortable with themselves emotionally. When a wife opens the oven door and discovers that her cake is burnt to a crisp, she will quickly straighten up with dismay on her face and say accusingly, "If your mother hadn't kept interrupting me while I was watching it, this wouldn't have happened." She is simply rationalizing her failure with the cake. And it might work, too, unless her husband sees through the gambit.

"Look," he might say softly, "you forgot to turn the timer on. Mother didn't have anything to do with it. She called after you put the cake in." And after a moment's hesitation she might admit ruefully, "Well, it *could* have been your mother's fault, I suppose, but it isn't—it's mine. It's impossible to ruin a cake when you use a mix, but I sure did it." Normal people rationalize, but once confronted with the reality of a situation, they are capable of moving back through the rationalization to the reality with relative ease. The normal, not too defensive person finally accepts the blame. But the alcoholic cannot make this trip back to reality. He cannot take the blame upon himself. The rationalization is an almost pick-proof lock.

As the process of alcoholism continues, repeated shameful, painful, unpredictable, and compulsive patterns of behavior persist over a long period of time. And as they grow more painful and shameful, rationalization rises to the challenge. The intellect continues to meet these onslaughts on sanity and to deflect them until the individual doing the rationalizing becomes victimized by the very process itself. In short, as time goes on he continues to *believe* more and more of the fairly plausible parts of these efforts to restore his sense of dignity and self-worth. The ultimate general effect is to draw him quite literally out of touch with reality.

The time comes when he can sit in the counselor's office and declare with absolute sincerity, "I don't have a drinking problem. Everything's fine at home and at the office. Like everybody else, I drink a little socially, but my problem is migraine headaches." And he literally believes that what, by any objective measurement, would be viewed as blatantly false is in fact true. Thus one sees him put the problem somewhere else. Eventually, owing to the progress of the disorder and his continued bad behavior, he *must* deceive himself if he is to live with himself at all. Paradoxically, it is a matter of survival. As a result he becomes successfully self-deceiving and progressively self-deluded. The degree of his delusion is another index to the progress of the illness.

He is now drinking excessively from time to time. And after another episode, instead of his being simply uncomfortable about the drinking and the behavior that accompanies it, the emotional cost is greater and he has real feelings of remorse. We can chart on the graph the forces that cause rationalization to develop, and illustrate the distance he has slipped toward *pain.* He had reached point 2 on the graph, and if he could verbalize his feelings you might hear the following monolgue: "That was stupid last night! Nobody stands on a table and leads cheers at the club—"

Later on, he drinks excessively again and behaves more outrageously. This time his feelings register even more severe remorse (3 on the graph). His reaction is not "That was stupid," but "*I* was stupid last night. I'll have to call two people and apologize." His drinking and his consequent behavior are consistently driving feelings about self downward.*

Figure VII

PHASE THREE: HARMFUL DEPENDENCE

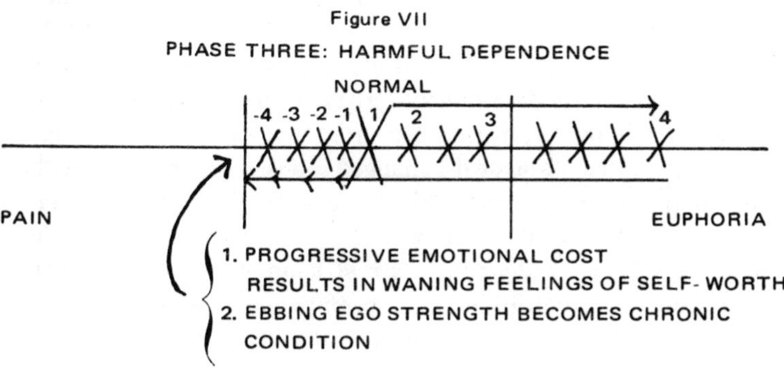

Still another drinking experience and the emotional reaction is even more painful. At point 4 on the Feeling Chart, he castigates himself: "I was a fool last night!" And so time passes and the condition develops. Over a period of months and years his self-image continues to wane. His ego strength ebbs. Down, down go his feelings of self-

*What is true here of alcohol seems clearly to be true of harmful dependency on all the "mood changing" chemicals. Indeed, the "pure alcoholic" is being replaced by the "pan" addict to minor tranquilizers, amphetamines, and barbiturarates as well as ethyl alcohol.

worth as continued excessive drinking goes on producing painful and bizarre behavior. At some point, this emotional distress becomes a chronic condition, i.e., he begins to feel the distress unconsciously even when he is *not drinking.* Now the very serious stages in the self-destructive process are at hand. He is swinging out of control. Drinking bouts begin to provide real self-hatred as an aftermath. "I'm just no damn good," he feels, and he has reached 5 in Figure VIII.

Now he begins to evidence "mood swings" or "personality changes" while drinking. The kind man becomes angry or hostile; the happy man becomes sad or morose; and the gentle man becomes violent. Alcohol is causing him to drop his guard, and the chronic unconscious negative feelings are exposed. The sequel to this condition, which is not long coming, is truly self-destructive. (see 6 in Fig. VIII). And the drinking itself may—occasionally and unexpectedly—continue to oblivion. The pattern is that he will drop in "only for a drink or two" after work, and stay until the place closes. Or he brings home a bottle, planning to have a couple of drinks during the evening. But when he wakes up in the morning, the bottle is empty. During this stage, all the so-called "geographical cures" may be considered or even tried.

All this drinking and emotional distress may lead to a vague but poignant feeling that "a problem" exists. There is a general malaise so strongly felt that desperate measures to escape are proposed or actually attempted. "Maybe if I changed spouses, or jobs, or cities this whole thing would clear up!" This is frequently the feeling, and some sort of erratic action may follow.

The final stages of alcoholism are at hand (see 7 in Fig. VIII). Continued excessive drinking and accompanying behavior bring on chronic suicidal feelings. Self-appraisal runs: "I'm no damn good. I'm so rotten, I might as well end it all." Drinking or not drinking, suicidal thoughts start flashing through the mind. When driving, it's "At 65 mph, all I'd have to do is flip the wheel and that bridge abutment would take care of everybody's problem—including mine"; or down at the office, "This is high enough—all I have to do is lean out a little farther." Or a typical temptation might be just to forget to open the garage doors in the morning and let the motor run.

If the course of the disease is not interrupted, the end of all this is suicide, either slowly with the chemical alcohol, or in a more direct but equally final fashion. Point 8 is the last stop on the Feeling Chart.

As emotional distress mounts and the deterioration of personality

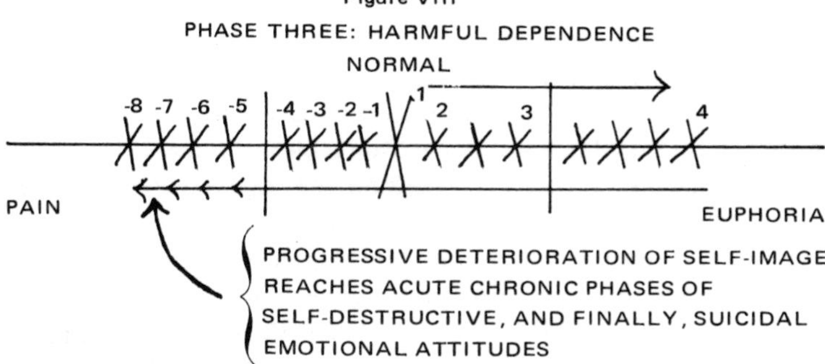

accelerates, there are all sorts of behavioral changes. To begin with, let us consider what happens when the counselor first questions the drinker to determine whether or not there is a pathological use of alcohol. Questions like:

"Have you ever drunk in the morning?"
"Have you ever drunk alone?"
"Have you ever drunk a fifth a day?"
"Have you ever felt remorse after drinking?"

are not only reasonable, they are the classic questions. If they were answered truthfully, it would be clear whether or not there has been a departure from social drinking. But such questions have now been abandoned. It has long been apparent that no one who is alcoholic can answer them accurately about himself. It is not so much that he is unwilling (although he is), but that he is indeed incapable of answering them factually. Thus it is impossible to find out from the subject himself what his behavior is.

Counselors have to use other methods to determine whether a harmful dependency is present. Nowadays they get a history of the behavior patterns of the drinker from the immediate and meaningful people around him rather than from the subject himself. The basic question is whether there has been a *changing life-style* around the use of alcohol which would indicate a *growing dependence.* They look for certain evidence. First, one might ask if there is a growing anticipation of the welcome effect of alcohol. Has it moved from anticipation to a *preoccupation?*

Preoccupation is hard to measure—it is a subjective consideration. However, when a person becomes alcoholic, preoccupation is there and must be taken into account. Why a person becomes preoccupied, and why this condition intensifies, again is still a mystery. How it develops is relatively clear from an examination of the life-style that is changing to adapt to it.

To illustrate, let's say that our man, having learned the basic lessons in Phase One (alcohol always gives him a pleasant mood swing), and having gone into Phase Two (seeking the mood swing), now has entered our drinking culture. During the second phase he uses the drug in an acceptable way so far as society is concerned. But he has come to realize that alcohol is a powerful agent to be used with certain limitations. So he searches out and adopts for himself a set of rules for drinking. These are self-imposed rules, mind you, and he lives by them successfully for a given time. One such rule, let's say, is the "five o'clock rule." "I'll stick to business during the day, or whatever I'm doing," he says. "I won't take a drink until five o'clock. Whatever drinking I do will be after five, even on my days off."

And he abides by the rule successfully for a period of his life. But the day comes, eventually, when he looks at his watch and discovers that it is only 2 P.M. There are three whole hours before release from the pain of existence is going to be socially available—a whole afternoon to go! His unspoken, fervent feeling is, "Gosh, it's going to feel good to go home and crawl around a dry martini tonight!" And he really suffers the pinch of waiting. Or, on his day off, he may begin to think more and more about what a day off should really mean. After all, such days are for "relaxing," and he knows how to relax. Life's hard enough without tormenting yourself. So why not have one or two while watching the big game on television. Now, that does the trick.

Gradually and imperceptibly, he adapts his rules and his life-style to indulge this *growing* feeling of anticipation of the welcome effect, until he is drinking at noon or even in the morning. He passes off this change in life-style as an adaption to his culture, without recognizing his predicament at all. "Everybody else is doing it. Why shouldn't I?" The plain truth is that he has been changing his own self-imposed rules to a point where they are entirely different from what they originally were. Ultimately they may even cease to exist.

The second symptom the counselors look for within the changing life-style is *rigidity*. Is there a growing rigidity about the times our subject is used to drinking, and how is this expressed in his behavior? Particularly, is there less and less adaptability when some unexpected intrusion upon these times occurs?

To take a familiar instance, let us say that our drinking man comes home after a day's work, and his wife meets him with a bulletin: "Remember," she says, "I have that meeting tonight. Supper's at six o'clock—that's right now. So wash up." There is a moment of silence.

Back in the good days, or Phase Two, when 'old hard-day-at-the-office' had no real dependency on alcohol, he would have been irritated and disappointed. But he would have fairly cheerfully put down his expectations, and hustled upstairs. Nobody likes to rush to the table, but so it goes. After all, his wife had told him that morning and he had forgotten.

However, some whiskey has gone over the dam since then. It is a different scene. We hear all the evidence of harmful dependency in his reponse to this change of signals. Predictably, his attitude is: "What do you mean 'right now'? What time is the meeting? You didn't tell me what time the meeting was."

"Well, I did tell you. I have to be at church at seven o'clock."

"But they don't meet until eight usually," he says accusingly.

"Well, they do tonight. There's a special service at eight."

"I was thinking about something else when you told me. You didn't really stop me and tell me. Look, it's six o'clock now. You mean we gotta eat right now?"

"Otherwise your dinner's going to be cold."

"Well, what have you got?" he asks belligerently.

"I fixed a chicken."

"I can't eat a cold chicken."

"No—so you'll have to eat now."

"You're telling me I've got to sit down and eat a chicken right now?"

"That's what I told you this morning."

"Can I bring a drink to the table?"

"Why do you always have to have a drink?" she asks exasperatedly.

"I had that conference this morning, and—well, it's been tough going. I've had a hard day."

"I'm sure you've had a hard day, but this one time I do have a meeting, and let's eat."

"Why don't you forget the church tonight?"

"You know I can't do that. I'm president of the Altar Guild."

"Yeah, but isn't one of those other jackass ladies able to pick this thing up and run with it?"

"This is an important meeting of the Guild. I've told you all that. I've got the report and I've got to run the meeting."

"Boy, you know if you ran the house and forgot about the damn church, the church might run itself. But, there are damn few people around that'll run the house."

"I understand how you feel, but you were perfectly agreeable this morning when I told you about it!"

"Well," he says, "you know how it is—I never anticipate. You just eat your chicken now, and I'm going to have a drink. I'll eat mine cold, later, and you go on to the church and I hope everything works out great at the meeting."

This same sort of scene will be played in variation, endlessly. The unexpected change in routine intruded upon his expected drinking time. This sort of rigidity becomes more and more pervasive, until he actually plans his whole day around drinking occasions. Even the most important business meetings will be slipped into the lunch schedule: "Let's discuss that at lunch where we won't be interrupted by the phone," he says.

There is a third sign for which counselors are alert in examing the changing life-style. They try to find evidence of a growing tolerance of the chemcial.

Does it take more alcohol for the drinker to get the same welcome effect? Is he drinking in the kitchen before he brings the other drinks in—having a little shooter to warm up? And to what lengths is he willing to go to get the extra volume of alcohol it takes to give him that same feeling? The degree of ingenuity used to get more becomes the scale for determining the progress of the dependency.*

There is always the sudden panic when our man comes home from work and is reminded that they are going to dinner at the Smiths. A panic, because at the Smiths they have one drink before dinner and that's it. He knows he can't get that old feeling from one drink, or even two. "The Smiths," he repeats to himself with rising alarm, and makes a quick detour by the home bottle and pours himself "one" to drink while he is dressing.† "Doesn't everybody?" he asks himself. He sees himself exhibiting real forethought in preparing for an "unnatural" drinking situation. And when he arrives at the Smiths, he is a wizard at self-reliance. The one drink is soon gone, and he is sitting there

*Apparently there is also the breakdown of this tolerance. Overreactions occur unpredictable from time to time. On some occasions, relatively small amounts of alcohol may cause intoxication; on others, large amounts do not.

†One drink can be anything—a glass of any size containing any amount. The jigger eventually disappears from use.

clinking his ice cubes. He is signaling Smith, sort of hopelessly, while he waits for a chance to break the drought. It comes. The doorbell rings announcing late arrivals. As Smith goes forward to receive them, our man makes his pitch. He says brightly, "I'll fix the drinks for the Turnbulls—I know what they want." And he is away for a couple of quick shooters, and another drink for himself to "keep the Turnbulls company." "I knew you wouldn't want to drink alone," he says, "so I fixed myself a little dividend just to keep you company!"

This is skill in maneuver rather than ingenuity in hiding bottles, which art shows up soon enough. As surveillance of our friend increases, he becomes enormously cunning in hitting upon hiding places for his liquor—finding unnoticed but always available nooks, crannies, and containers becomes no problem at all.

There is astonishing universality about the hiding places people pick. Past and present, they stash bottles away in the same places they always have, though occasionally a real instance of ingenuity shows up. One case that came to the attention of the Johnson Institute involved a man who had sworn off alcohol in the presence of his family, his doctor, and everybody. The family kept an eye on him, though, and would sort of stick with him when he moved about. One unseasonably warm day, he told his wife that he was going into the back yard to get a little sunburn. A laudable project. So he stretched out on the back lawn in full view of the kitchen where his wife was working.

Now he was out in the yard and perfectly visible to everybody, including his very attentive wife, and for that period his family was entirely relaxed. About two hours later he came in, drunker than a skunk. They could not figure it out. It was subsequently revealed that he had filled a coke bottle with gin and buried it the night before. He smuggled out a straw, and all he had to do was slip it in the bottle and begin sucking. Every time he turned on his stomach to get some sun on his back, which was frequently, he had a deep drag on the gin, and soon felt just fine.

Thus all the instances of harmful dependency that turn up in the behavior patterns of the alcoholic in Phase Three indicate a maladaptation of the life-style to (a) growing anticipation of the welcome effect, (b) an increasing rigidity around the expected time of use, and (c) a progressive ingenuity in obtaining larger and larger amounts of alcohol.

3.

Rational Defenses and Projection

"It's somebody else's problem"

The obvious question at this point is, "Why don't these people see what is happening to them and quit drinking?" Since alcoholism is the third largest health problem in our country today, directly affecting between ten and twenty million people, the question is being asked by many millions of persons in these very words.

However, as one might expect, it is the wrong question. Almost all the questions we have asked alcoholics or asked about them have been wrong. If you drop "and quit drinking" from this inquiry, then you get to the real question: *"Why don't they see what is happening to them?"*

The answer is, they can't. They can't, and what is worse, many of those immediately around them can't either. That is, they cannot really *see* what is happening, either to these chemically dependent people or to themselves, as the disease progresses.

The reason the alcoholic is unable to perceive what is happening to him is understandable. As his condition develops, his self-image continues to deteriorate and his ego strength ebbs. For many reasons, he is progressively unable to keep track of his own behavior and is losing contact with his emotional self. His defense systems continue to grow, so that he can survive in the face of his problems. The greater the pain he suffers, the higher and more rigid the defenses become; and this whole process is unconscious. The alcoholic does not know what is happening inside of himself. Finally, he actually becomes a victim of his own defense mechanisms.

Alcoholic rationalizations have already been described. As the emotional turmoil grows in the chemically dependent person, his rational defense activity turns into real *mental mismanagement,* which serves to erect a secure wall (see Fig. IX) around these increasingly negative feelings he has about himself. The end result is that he is walled away from those feelings and becomes largely unaware that such destructive emotions exist within him. Not only is he unaware of his highly developed defense system; he is also unaware of the powerful feelings of self-hate buried behind it, sealed off from conscious knowledge, but explosively active. Because of this, his judgment is progressively impaired—and impaired judgment, by definition, does not know it is impaired.

Figure IX

PHASE THREE: HARMFUL DEPENDENCE (RATIONAL DEFENSES)

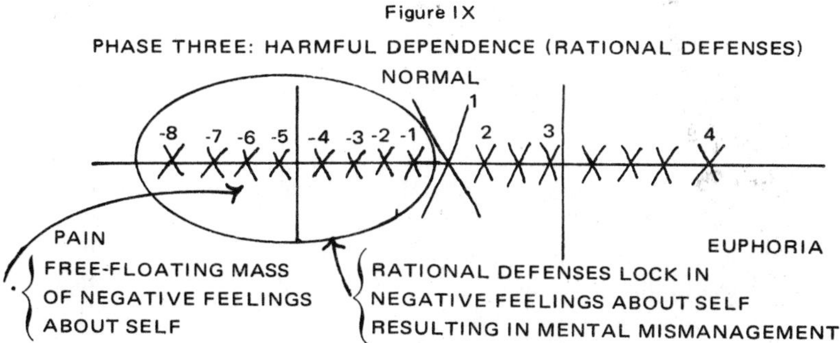

Morever, the problem is being compounded by the fact that these defenses, by locking in the negative feelings, have now created a mass of *free-floating anxiety, guilt, shame,* and *remorse* which becomes chronically present. This poisonous load is shown in the circle in Figure IX. To put it one way, this person is no longer emotionally able to start any given drinking episode from the "normal point" (1), where before his illness he could always start, and then swing up in mood to feel "good"(3), or "great" (4). Now he must start from where he is on the depressed or painful side of the graph and drink to feel *normal.* He is now in the fourth and final stage of alcoholism, in which the subject drinks to feel normal.

He is now deeply into all the increasingly ominous symptoms of deterioration, but probably still has his job, since this seems to be the last part of the alcoholic's life to deteriorate. In this state, if he has an important appointment for a business conference at 11:00 A.M.,

Figure X
PHASE FOUR: DRINKS TO FEEL NORMAL

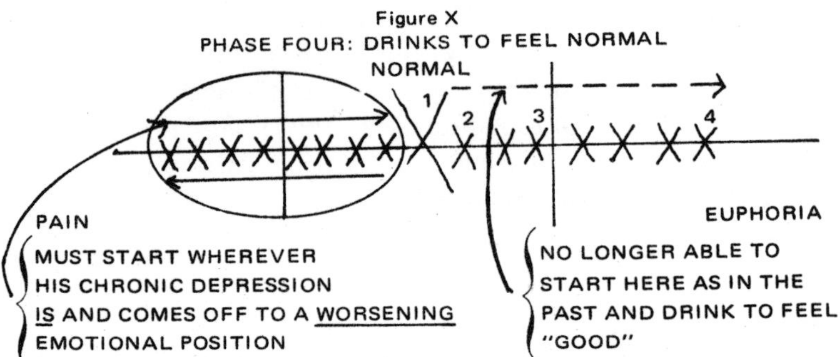

what he is going to do at 10:00 A.M. is a forgone conclusion: he will stop in at the bar around the corner for two "quick ones" so he can function as he knows he must at 11 o'clock.

We shall indicate the early and later signs of alcoholism on the job by means of the next chart, but when these symptoms appear, one can be resonably sure that many other problems have already arisen because of his drinking. The problem drinker is often able to conceal his illness on the job after his personal life is a shambles. Even though his marriage may be in serious trouble, his spouse will help him conceal the disease from his employer for fear he may lose his job.

The alcoholic himself is more responsive to his boss than he is to his family. And that means that the highest value in our American culture is placed on productivity. It is a bad deal, but it seems true of both the spouse and the alcoholic that the last thing they want destroyed is the job. Observe how this works in any alcoholic situation. The job is the spouse's status symbol and often more important to her than her husband's person or his spirit. Typically, she will hide from the boss the real home situation. She will say it is fine when it is actually in ruins (the whole thing can be destructive to a point that is unbelievable), and will assure him that things are going okay. Loss of the job is the last thing she wants.

We had a call from a law firm on Wall Street, and they told us, "We're just about to take on a partner who has left another big firm.

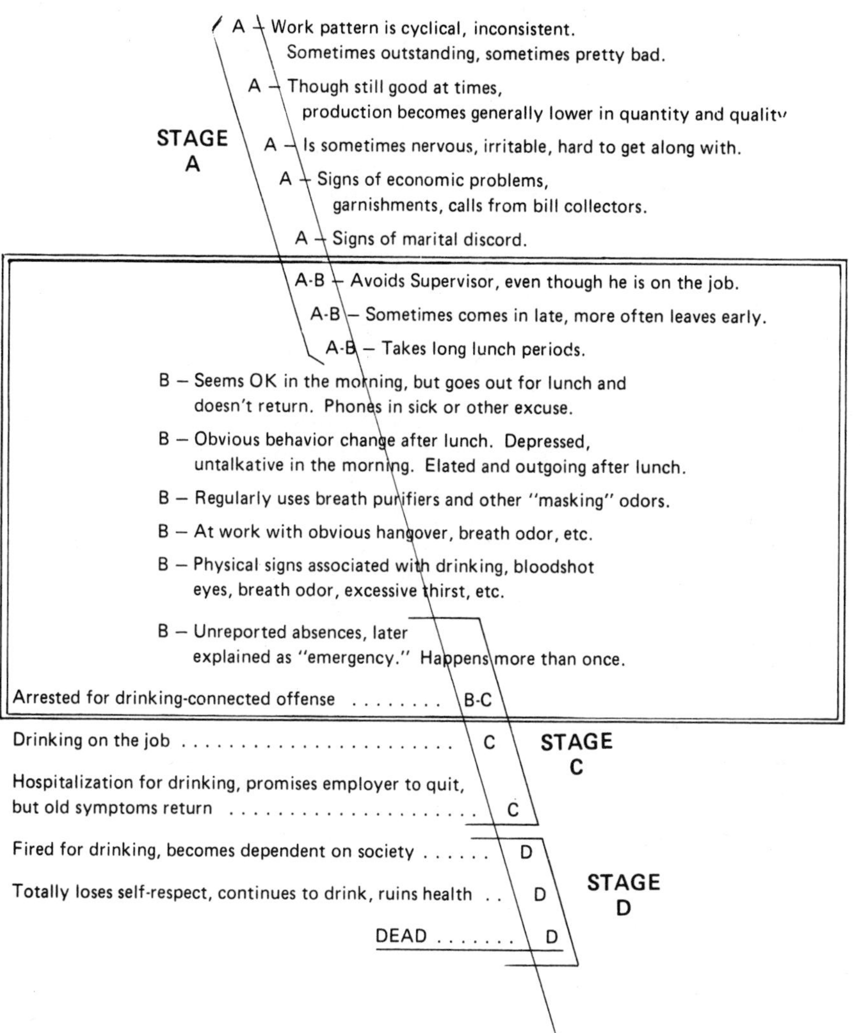
A – Work pattern is cyclical, inconsistent.
Sometimes outstanding, sometimes pretty bad.
A – Though still good at times,
production becomes generally lower in quantity and quality
STAGE A
A – Is sometimes nervous, irritable, hard to get along with.
A – Signs of economic problems,
garnishments, calls from bill collectors.
A – Signs of marital discord.
A-B – Avoids Supervisor, even though he is on the job.
A-B – Sometimes comes in late, more often leaves early.
A-B – Takes long lunch periods.
B – Seems OK in the morning, but goes out for lunch and
doesn't return. Phones in sick or other excuse.
B – Obvious behavior change after lunch. Depressed,
untalkative in the morning. Elated and outgoing after lunch.
B – Regularly uses breath purifiers and other "masking" odors.
B – At work with obvious hangover, breath odor, etc.
B – Physical signs associated with drinking, bloodshot
eyes, breath odor, excessive thirst, etc.
B – Unreported absences, later
explained as "emergency." Happens more than once.
STAGE B
Arrested for drinking-connected offense . . . . B-C
Drinking on the job C
STAGE C
Hospitalization for drinking, promises employer to quit,
but old symptoms return C
Fired for drinking, becomes dependent on society . . . . . . D
Totally loses self-respect, continues to drink, ruins health . . D
STAGE D
DEAD . . . . D

We're a little concerned because there is a rumor around the street that the reason for his leaving was alcohol." We said we'd be glad to help. The lawyer finally ended up at the Johnson Institute in Minneapolis with his wife. After our evaluation, he was perfectly agreeable to entering treatment. And she absolutely refused to let him. She accepted the fact that he was sick, but reasoned that treatment would corroborate the real reason for the dissolution of the previous relationship. It would confirm the rumors as to why he had left. They had been brushing them aside. It didn't matter what he said—whether he lived or died or anything else—she was protecting the image of his being a top man on Wall Street.

Now the alcoholic drinks because he has been drinking. As the Chinese say, "First the man takes a drink, and then the drink takes a drink, and finally the drink takes the man." At this stage, his drinking pattern becomes thoroughly unpredictable or compulsive. He quits and he resumes, and does not know why he has begun drinking again. And whenever he does start again, the resumption is at the level of the chronic emotional deterioration. His condition worsens with each new episode. Rather than being caught in a vicious circle, he is trapped in a downward, deadly spiral.

As the mass of free-floating negative feelings inside him grows, locked in now by the wall of effective rational defenses, the weight of it becomes ever more difficult to bear. Sooner or later, the chemically dependent person must resort—unconsciously again—to the one other powerful system of defense that is available to him: projection.

Projecting is the process of unloading self-hate onto those around you. Again the alcoholic does not know this is happening; it occurs unconsciously. The more hateful the alcoholic unconsciously sees himself to be, the more he will come to see himself as surrounded by hateful people. "They are always trying to run my life." or "They are messing things up and making it harder for me!" Depending upon his overall personality and his immediate moods, he does this projecting in a variety of ways from passive, even gentle complaining to blazing aggression. In any case, he must dump this load of self-hatred in order to survive.

The people around the alcoholic, the most meaningful and the handiest, are the objects of the greatest part of his projecting. The message he sends them by whatever means is: "If you would straighten up, I'd be all right!" It is really himself that he hates, but projection works so well—just as the other defenses do—that he actually believes that those he attacks are hateful people. He *must* see it that way, for if he knew he was projecting it would not work for him. The process must remain unconscious.

There is a further complicating factor. The people around an alcoholic, being human, are vulnerable. They know that something is terribly wrong, but since they do not understand what is going on—that he is projecting his own self-hatred—they frequently feel guilty when he dumps his load. They ask themselves, "What did *I* do to bring this on?"

Figure XI

PHASE THREE AND FOUR: HARMFUL DEPENDENCE (PROJECTION)

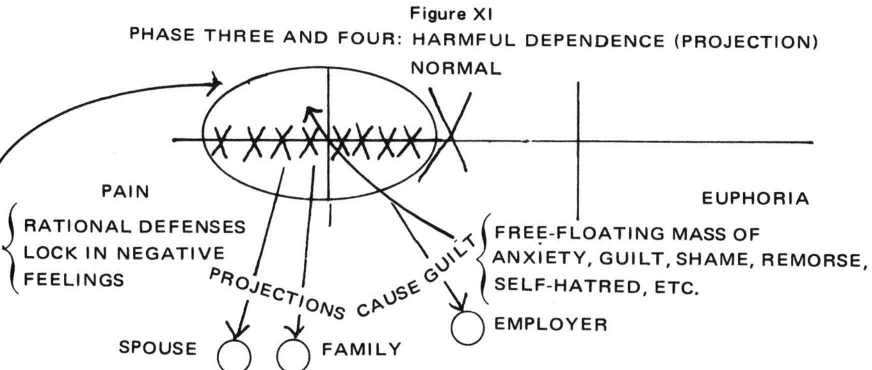

Out of feelings of guilt, the victims of projection begin to manipulate. They try to correct the situation, and the following patterns of behavior result. They fix dinner late, they fix dinner early. They "cooperate" in every possible way. They cajole, they wheedle; they beg, they flash back in anger. They make sure the liquor supply is there; they pour the bottles down the kitchen sink. Whatever they try (they inevitably discover) *does not work.* The situation worsens. They become more anxious and guilty, and attempt even more frantic manipulations. As their failures mount in number, their feelings of inadequacy grow, making them still more vulnerable to projections. They too become emotionally distressed, often as severely as the chemically dependent person himself. This means that every sick alcoholic is surrounded by other sick nonalcoholics. In view of this, one may wonder what disease is "first" in America today.

"Alcoholism *includes* alcoholics," is a way of stating the breadth of the problem area. While there may be only one alcoholic in a family, the whole family suffers from the alcoholism. For every harmfully dependent person, most often there are two, three, or even more people immediately around him who are just as surely victims of the disease. They too need real help and should be included in any thoroughgoing model of therapy. Of course the spouse is particularly involved. The only difference between the alcoholic and the spouse, in instances where the latter does not drink, is that one is physically affected by alcohol; otherwise both have all the other symptoms. The dry is as sick as the drunk, except that the bodily damage is not there. With every drunk there is a sick dry who is almost a mirror image.

The people around the alcoholic person have predictable experiences that are psychologically damaging. As they meet failure after failure, their feelings of fear, frustration, shame, inadequacy, guilt, resentment, self-pity, and anger mount, and so do their defenses. They too use rationalization as a defense against these feelings because they are threatened with a growing sense of self-worthlessness. They too begin to project these masses of free-floating negative feelings about themselves upon the children, back on the spouse, on other family members, on employees, and everybody else at hand. Their defenses have begun to operate in the same way as the alcoholic's, although they are unconscious of this, and they are also victimized by their defenses rather than helped. Out of touch with reality, just like the alcoholic, they say, "*I* don't need help. It's his problem, not mine!" The chemically dependent and those around him all have impaired judgment; they differ only in the degree of impairment.

The person who is chemically dependent on alcohol has such a highly developed defense system that he becomes seriously self-deluded. The rigid defenses which have risen spontaneously around his negative feelings about himself,* and therefore around the behaviors that caused these feelings, would be quite enough, were they the

*Not only are these defenses becoming more and more rigid, but the individual develops a growing rigidity in his very life-style. It is characteristic that he is less and less able to adapt to changes in his environment, particularly to any unexpected change. Paradoxically, he reaches a point later when even schedules are burdensome to him. He is less and less likely to plan ahead. Or when he does plan, he tends to feel trapped as the moment for carrying out the activity approaches. "Why did I agree to do that tonight? I really would rather not go." He is rigidly locked into a pattern of life he cannot recognize as being present.

only deluding factors, to draw him progressively and thoroughly out of touch with reality. When he passes into harmful dependency, he reaches a point where it is not a question of whether he will see what is happening to him, but rather whether he *can*. In due time, he *cannot*.

4.

Blackouts, Repression, and Euphoric Recall

"I was perfectly all right"

We have explained how the alcoholic's highly developed defense system keeps him out of touch with reality. Rationalization, projection, and denial even make it impossible for him to understand that he has a drinking problem. People seeing this most often think he is lying. From the outside, it appears that the truth is being flouted by someone who is still responsible to that truth and entirely able to know it. These pathological impairments are devastating, but there is an even more bewildering set of forces that afflicts the alcoholic. Three progressive conditions attack his memory system. Blackouts, repression, and euphoric recall destroy the chemically dependent person's ability to remember accurately what has happened on any given drinking occasion.

The blackout may come late in the development of the disease. Not to be confused with "passing out" or drinking to the point of losing consciousness, the chemically induced blackout involves a permanent and complete loss of memory for a given period of time. The victim goes on functioning during the blackout as if he were aware of what was going on around him and would remember everything that happened. Actually, he remembers none of it ever again. These are real periods of amnesia. To add to the confusion, other people present during the blackouts perceive the alcoholic to be normal and assume that he is in control of his faculties. They resume relations with him, following these memory lapses, on the assumption that they have shared a common experience. The victim is generally so embarrassed by his loss of memory that he tries to bluff it out. Enormous confusion is likely to ensue.

As the illness progresses, blackouts become more frequent, of longer duration, and more unpredictable as far as the amount of alcohol necessary to induce them is concerned. The time will come when a relatively small amount may cause a blackout, or inversely, large amounts may not. In any case, after blackouts the victim is haunted by such questions as:

"How did I get home last night—?"
"Did I hurt anybody—?"
"Where did I leave my car—?"
"What did I do last night after 10:00 P.M.—?"
"Who was I with? Did I make a fool of myself?"
"Did I make a pass at my host's wife?"
"Where am I? How did I get into this hotel room in this strange city?"

The morning after a severe blackout, it is a common experience for the victim tremulously to check the front bumper of his car for signs of collision or even blood stains.

A counselor at the Johnson Institute had an experience which illustrates how complex a blackout can be. An old college friend unexpectedly dropped by late one afternoon—a judge in a distant county of the state, whom the counselor had not seen for a number of years. As the judge sat down, the impression was that he was well dressed and that he walked and talked well. He smelled a little of alcohol. "Gosh, I'm really upset!" he began, as he took an airplane ticket envelope out of his pocket. "This ticket says I've been to Rome, Italy and back, and I don't remember being there! I was on my way to Kansas City four days ago. I'm scared."

The counselor questioned him briefly about his drinking during the week and received admissions of it, but the answers were vague. "You have good reason to be worried, all right," the counselor told him. "You've been in a severe blackout, so severe that I suspect you've had a number of such incidents before!"

The friend nodded, "Yeah, a few times I guess, but never like this. I'm thoroughly frightened. Imagine! Rome, Italy!"

The counselor began to explain the significant implications of blacking out with reference to the disease concept, and since he noted close attention and appropriate concern, he continued for the greater part of an hour to describe thoroughly the brain syndrome as a whole. He concluded with, "I don't really need to know your past drinking history in detail. What I do know is that you're in trouble *now,* and the real question is, can you quit drinking? I mean, are you so dependent you can't stop by yourself?"

"Oh I can stop, I'm sure. I have, several times in the last ten years. I can do it!"

He had not realized how much he was revealing in that one short sentence. The problem was there, and it had been progressing for *at least ten years!* People who vow to quit have been given reason to do so. But the counselor had a sudden thought, since he knew the judge's wife well, too. "Does your wife know where you are?"

The friend looked uncomfortable. "I guess she does, because I usually call home frequently when I'm away. I must have called, but to be truthful, I don't remember!"

The counselor urged him to call immediately. "She might be terribly distressed." The call was made, and what he overheard of it caused the counselor to suggest that the friend go home as quickly as possible to straighten things out. He recommended that the judge return with her the next day so that "we can go right to work on this very serious problem." And then he asked, "How will you get home?"

The judge called a friend with a private airplane who agreed to fly him home without delay. "Since it's an emergency, I can do it," said the friend, "If you'll meet me at the airport right now." The judge called a taxi and left, promising to drive back the next day with his wife. Soon after his departure, a secretary informed the counselor that a cab driver was in the waiting room looking for the judge. "They've sent two cabs," said the counselor. "I'll come out and explain."

As he was telling the driver that the judge had already left by taxi, the driver shook his head and said, "I don't understand it! I dropped him off here two hours ago with his instructions that I return now to pick him up. I have his luggage in my cab."

Only then did the counselor realize that his friend had been in a blackout while he was in the office. He would finally come back to the world of memory somewhere, with not only an inexplicable plane ticket in his pocket, but the counselor's office appointment card as well. He would not be able to recall either event.

Note the confusions compounded in this extreme incident. First, there is the judge who would have no recollection of several days of his life. He would not remember where he had been or with whom. Nor would he be able to recall how much money he had spent (it turned out to be far too much) until the canceled checks and the credit card billings came on the first of the month. Days had dropped out of his life; yet no *specific* memories of them could return to tell him how sick he was getting.

The scene is further complicated by the judge's behavior in the counselor's office. Here his speech was appropriate and he had enough control so that the counselor, despite his expertise, was unable to detect the condition. He stumbled on the truth, in fact, only through his chance meeting with the cab driver. Without that, the counselor would have fully expected him to return with his wife the next day as planned. And he would have assumed, then, that they shared a clear memory of the two hours of work already accomplished. To repeat any of their earlier conversation at the second meeting would be repetitious and quite unnecessary.

But the truth was that he would not only have to repeat all the foregoing material, but would have to call long distance to reestablish the appointment for the second session itself!

And once more, confusion compounded! The judge had been appropriately worried about being in a blackout *while he was in a blackout!*

So extreme a situation, it should be noted, is relatively rare; though it did happen, and parallels to it continue to occur. Usually the blackout is much shorter and the behavior not so destructive. The man in our graph going through a typical blackout was probably losing only an hour or two, or even just a few minutes at a time. He was detected telling the same story to the same people in the same hour at parties. Nevertheless, with each of these episodes he became more fearful, bewildered, and depressed. (Again, of course, his defenses went to work, locking in these feelings so that the pain would not be unbearable.)

In any case, he was denied the opportunity to confront his own antisocial behavior. He could not even apologize appropriately. Shame, guilt, and self-reproach were vague and unattached, and therefore impossible to deal with though poignantly present. They simply increased the growing mass of free-floating anxiety (see circle on Fig. X). Our typical victim becomes more depressed. "I thought I was going crazy, so every time I blacked out I'd force myself to forget it. I got so good at this that I had myself actually believing things just slipped my mind from time to time!" Even the blackouts blacked out. He frequently did not remember they had occurred at all. His pattern of delusion deepened.

Dismaying as the judge's experience was, the records are full of more horrifying episodes. One morning I had a call from an acquaintance who was a real estate broker in town. "Vern," he said in a far-away, shocked tone of voice, "you can't believe it. They tell me that last night I drove my car through three kids on bicycles and killed one. I don't remember it." The night before his trial he committed suicide.

Obviously, a blackout is enormously disruptive in the conduct of business, and alcoholic businessmen discover that more than simple embarrassment is involved when a loss of memory affects a vital transaction. In interviews at the Johnson Institute we hear many descriptions of such incidents in the process of getting the data that make it possible for us to judge the degree of alcoholic dependency. Frequently the meaningful person who comes to us along with the alcoholic—the wife or husband or whoever—will provide the information that blackouts have occurred. This may come out after the counselor has described the disease of alcoholism and asked the wife or the partner the standard question: "I'd like to ask you, Mrs. Smith, in my description do you see anything with which you identify?"

"Oh, my gosh, you just told me my husband's life! I never talked to you before and you just described him to a T."

He says, "Yeah, well, there are a couple of places all right. But . . ."

She says, "Well, how about the blackouts?"

"Well, a couple of . . ."

"How about last Tuesday night?" she challenges him directly. The counselor picks this up and says, "Yeah, how about Tuesday night?"

"Well, he came home already loaded, and he just drank all into the evening. And there was a phone call at 10 o'clock—a very important business call. And I learned on Wednesday that he had forgotten entirely, the whole thing. It was a ten-minute call, and he forgot the whole thing. It was really a costly business that he forgot, because that was one of his key clients."

"Well, I didn't forget that," he says defensively, and she nails him.

"I know you forgot it. Don't kid me. Because I got a call Wednesday afternoon saying where were you, that you were supposed to be at this place at 2 P.M."

And when he tries to give her a big story about how he was busy, she says, "I was there listening to your half of the conversation, and you told him two o'clock at such and such a place, and I'll be there, and this is a $10,000 deal, and we'll make it and . . ." All facts were there.

The poor guy said finally, "Well, I've had a couple of those."

This sort of blackout—that is, losing a telephone conversation—will be much more familiar to the average alcoholic than taking a trip to Rome. But regardless of the duration, whether days or minutes, physiologically it is the same phenomenon and very serious.

A blackout is dramatic and ominous, but the alcoholic's unconscious use of *repression* contributes more to his distorted view of himself and his worsening condition. All persons, of course, unconsciously repress unwanted, shameful, or painful memory material from time to time. It is a mechanism provided to everyone, and in a sense at least is what keeps people sane. If a fifty-year-old man could and did remember in a single moment of time *all* his shameful and painful acts in a half-century of living, he would go into an irreversible emotional collapse. He simply could not bear such a burden—it would turn him into a gibbering idiot forthwith. Normal and sane people exist and remain so because they do not have that many such events to remember; at least a significant portion of them are turned off or tuned out. It is quite another matter, however, when the actions producing pain and shame are *repeated* time and again, and worsen with the passage of time, with their memory frequently repressed as occurs with alcoholism.*

As to the delusions produced by repression, one incident in the life of the man on the chart will serve to illustrate the hundreds of others.

It was morning. His eyes opened, and he saw a ceiling. *His* ceiling! He was in the right place! His first feeling was relief. Then he made the effort to get out of bed, and it was an effort, because last night was last night. It was just yesterday morning that he promised his wife, himself, and God it would never happen again! Next came a flood of sheer horror. Notice that he did not remember the details of the night before; just that it *was*. Two alternatives were then open to him. Either the horror would be allowed to remain conscious, and all the specific recalling of which he was capable would follow, or the whole thing had to be turned off. All this, of course, was dealt with instinctively in a split second. His mind was already at work in another direction.

*This is the other side of the coin. What the alcoholic does remember of his past haunts him fiercely. He is told on all sides, by well-meaning friends, "You have to forget the past!" He replies poignantly, "Yes, but how?" What he does remember depresses him, but what he cannot remember keeps him deluded about his condition.

"Just twelve minutes to go through the bathroom routine, shave, and dress to go to the office." As he stood at the mirror whittling away at his beard, specific memories occurred. Each, upon arrival in the mind, was snipped off successfully. "Got to get to work!" was the refrain that won the day. And so, twelve minutes later, he reached the top of the stairs, put a smile on his lips (an effort at first), and by the time he reached the bottom step was actually whistling a merry tune. "It's another day, and another dollar." The repression of last night and its events was complete.

But then he came into the breakfast area, and there it was! That angry and thoroughly resentful face on the other side of the table. *She* knew last night was last night! His reaction to the sight was typical. He felt neither shame nor guilt nor remorse. The repression was too thoroughgoing. This woman of his choice, this mother of his children aroused his genuine wonder and real concern. He leaned over her solicitously and asked softly, "Is something bugging you this morning?" She dashed from the room in shocked tears, and he left the house bewildered at the antics of forty-year-old women. She appeared in the counselor's office later, wringing her hands, asking, "Am I going crazy? I must be, because *nobody* could look that cool, that calm, and that collected and have last night *be* last night! Maybe it didn't happen?"

She was told about blackouts and the power of repression.

By multiplying such episodes, one can gain a perspective of this man's growing delusion. "I had my own built-in blackout system and it worked." Whole areas of his life were quite literally forgotten as his illness progressed, even though they were not chemically blacked out. His memory did not in any way help him to realize the growing severity of his symptoms. In fact, the more bizarre the behavior pattern, the stronger became the instinct to repress. Recurrent depression resulted. Nervousness, resentment, hostility, and self-pity intensified, and chronic depression deepened. (see again the circle on the chart (Fig. VIII).

It is obvious how disrupting and damaging blackout and repression are as they progressively separate the alcoholic from the reality of his behavior. And yet the third condition that distorts the memory system —*euphoric recall*—must be the most devastating. This term describes how the alcoholic remembers every one of his excessive drinking episodes: that is, euphorically or happily. There is no time when he has been under the influence that he is able to recall accurately, and yet he goes on believing firmly that he remembers everything in complete detail. This type of distortion is vitally important because it involves all the drinker's antisocial and destructive behavior.

The average cocktail party offers an opportunity to observe how ethyl alcohol works on consciousness and memory. At your next cocktail party, don't drink. Observe. Let's say you have just arrived with the other guests, and they are all normal human beings—nobody has had a drink yet.

You are served a drink. Typically, the first drink in our drinking culture will not perceptibly change any behavior whatsoever, because tolerance has risen so much. But with the second drink you will begin to notice several things happening. Early in the party there is a very intellectual response to booze. Usually all the great problems of the world are discussed and solved. The decibels will start rising. This is because alcohol affects the hearing, so that everybody hears less and talks louder. Then you will notice the quality of the tone changing from normal seriousness or quietness to the gay, the giddy, the laughing and joking. With the third drink the laughter is still louder—that's because alcohol has reached the part of the brain that controls inhibitions. Once inhibitions are relaxed, behavior changes. The effect of ethyl alcohol on any cell in the human body is to depress that cell. When the cells in the brain are depressed there is a less guarded, a gayer, more wide-open feeling. This is why alcohol looks like an "upper" when actually it's a depressant.

Then as the depression of the brain continues to the lower areas, the atmosphere changes from highly intellectual to emotional. The lower part of the brain houses our emotional lives: that's where we feel glad, sad, mad, etc. When there is a depression here you get the giggles, and jokes make the rounds—there is a kind of open emotionalism. It's a physiological progress, and that better be where the party stops. If the depression gets much lower it will affect breathing and heartbeat and that sort of thing.

Anybody who drinks enough so that he is really under the influence of alcohol is incapable of remembering accurately what he has said or done. When you get this repeatedly in the life of an alcoholic, where every time he drinks he gets drunk, or excessive drinking is in any sense a fixture, then on every one of these occasions he is incapable of remembering what went on. He gets this depression that relaxes his inhibitions, and what he remembers is that he felt good. He felt good, so it must have come off beautifully. "I had a few drinks, but I was perfectly all right. What's bugging them? Why can't they have fun drinking like I do?" And there he was weaving all over the place and spilling his drinks on the carpet. It isn't just that he has forgotten, it's that he didn't notice while it was happening. There is a distortion in perception here. We call this *euphoric recall.*

In every one of his excessive drinking episodes, he will be, the next day, only able to recall euphorically. That is, the chemical alcohol has affected his brain so that in no way can he remember his slurred words, or weaving gait, or exaggerated gesticulations, or broken sentences. His recollection is, "I was a terrific hit. Everybody loved me and I did just fine." This area of perception and memory distortion contributes powerfully to an alcoholic's inability to see and appreciate reality, and to his failure to recognize and accept the fact that he is on a downward spiral.

A typical experience might involve a visit to a friend's house for a couple of drinks. The scenario usually runs this way: After a drink or two a couple of times over, our friend has come to the end of the evening and prepares to drive home. The host actually suggests that maybe he has had one too many, and he'll be delighted to drive his guests home in his car, or theirs. "No problem," says our friend, weaving about. "I'm perfectly all right—I'll take my wife right home. Great time . . ." The friend insists and persists and finally prevails and drives them home. The next morning our one-way guests wake up, and the husband remembers exactly what happened the night before (or so he believes) and discusses it with his wife. "Tom overreacts to anybody who had two drinks. I was perfectly all right last night, but I thought I'd better humor him rather than make a scene."*

He says this not just to rationalize his behavior, but because he seriously and sincerely believes it. He trusts his euphoric recall implicitly. Later on, he may express his disbelief upon actually hearing a tape recording of one of his drinking episodes. Before playing the recording, his wife has asked him pointedly if he could remember *how* he had said what he said the night before. His reply is, "I had a few drinks, but I was perfectly all right." She turns on the machine, and disbelief, shock, and dismay register as he hears his own voice stuttering, stammering, and slurring through the virtually nonsensical sen-

*Notice that if the wife had a similar amount to drink and was herself under the influence, even though she saw and heard it all she would agree with him quite sincerely in the morning. "Yes, I knew you were all right, but I'm glad you didn't make a scene." Her memory would be equally distorted.

tences he has uttered only ten hours earlier.

"The really terrible feeling came when I realized how many times I remembered (quite clearly) just feeling good when I must have behaved the same way!" Only later could he recall the parties he had left, declaring that he had been the life of the party and believing it, while other guests were shaking their heads and saying, "If he's invited to the next party we're not coming."

The victim cannot understand why others look askance at him or even shun him after a while. Separation from previous relationships takes place from this time on, first the less meaningful and finally even the most valued. People cannot understand why he does not see what he is doing to himself and others. He cannot understand why they are avoiding him. Again the pattern of self-delusion deepens, and the lonely life begins.

In summary, then, in the chemically dependent person there are two groups of factors *progressively working together* to draw him out of touch with reality: his defense systems and his distortions of memory. Either one of these alone would seriously impair his judgment. The time inevitably comes when it is no longer relevant to ask whether he will see that he is sick; the plain fact is that he *cannot* see that he is sick. Yet he is acutely ill with a condition which will inevitably kill him and which will increasingly impair his constitution emotionally, mentally, and spiritually during his final months or years. A major part of his illness is a progressive emotional disorder which must be significantly reduced if he is to return to any kind of productive—not to mention happy—life. He is the victim of a constantly developing mental mismanagement, which if it progresses can result only in suicide. He needs the delivery of health care to his acute multiphasic health problem but he is not receiving it.

Two obstacles prevent the alcoholic from getting the attention he needs. First, most people are put off by his behavior because they do not understand his condition. They continue to approach him with disdain on their faces and scorn in their voices, demanding, "Why can't you see how sick you are getting?" This serves only to make him more isolated and more defensive. Or they wheedle him with, "If you loved me or the children you would have quit years ago." Thus they drive him deeper into feelings of self-pity and resentment. Or worse still, they turn their backs on him, in the fond but false expectation that somewhere, somehow, he will have a spontaneous insight. They even say sadly, "He just hasn't hit bottom yet."

The other reason he does not receive help is that he refuses to accept it because of his rigid defenses and distorted memory patterns. The sicker he gets, the more actively he resists intervention. He reaches the place where his fatty liver is becoming cirrhotic. His family is leaving; his job is in jeopardy. At this point his response remains, "Problem? What problem?"

It is quite obvious that his condition requires intervention *from the outside,* and it is equally obvious that only the more knowledgeable persons on the outside will be able to perform this function.

5.

The Dynamics of Intervention

Confrontation—the moment of reality

In approaching the problem of intervention with this disease, three basic factors must be taken into account. First, chemical dependency is a progressive illness. The physical symptoms appear and progress. The emotional symptoms appear and progress, and the mental mismanagement is increasingly destructive. Spiritual bankruptcy is the end result. "I'm just no damn good for me or anybody else!" Late treatment of this acute multiphasic disorder can be, and all too often is, *too late;* premature death occurs. Early intervention is a must. Earlier intervention means less destruction to the chemically dependent person's life and body. More important, it produces a greater likelihood of recovery.

The second factor is the chronic nature of the disease. The goal is not to "cure" but to arrest the illness. There is the ever-present danger of the "dry alcoholic" relapsing into destructive drinking patterns unless adequate measures are undertaken from the outset.* Again, because of the chronicity of the disease, *total abstinence* remains as the only logical or viable goal.

The third factor is that the disorder must be viewed as a *primary* condition. In due time it has its own specific symptomatology. Chemical dependency is especially primary from a practical viewpoint. It sits upon the individual in such a way that it blocks the lasting effect of any health care which might be delivered immediately to the physical,

*This is why aftercare is stressed so strongly in the hospitals. First comes three to four weeks of intensive impatient treatment of the acute physical, mental, and emotional phases, by a multidisciplined team of therapists. Then the patients enter a two-year outpatient program of rehabilitation which is designed to stabilize their sobriety.

emotional, or other complications. If there is a fatty liver, for example, nothing lasting can be done to reduce that condition until the dependency is lifted off. Allow the drinking to remain at abusive levels and the liver simply becomes more diseased until the damage is irreversible. If there is an existing emotional disorder, no lasting or effective therapy can be delivered until the dependency itself is corrected.*

The primary factor within this primary condition, however, is the delusion, or impaired judgment, which keeps the harmfully dependent person locked into his self-destructive pattern. It must be met and dealt with *first* (and on a continuing basis), since it blocks his entering any therapeutic process at all. The alcoholic evades or denies outright any need for help whenever he is approached. It must be remembered that he is not in touch with reality. But even at his sickest, he is capable of accepting some useful portion of reality, *if that reality is presented to him in forms he can receive.*

We may illustrate the dynamics of intervention with a case from the files of the Johnson Institute. A young clergyman came into the counselor's office one day and launched into an hour's description of his father's symptoms. It was clear that the father was in the late stages of alcoholism. "We must do something," the son said despairingly, "because not only is his life in danger, but more important, he's a physician and a surgeon. By now, other people's lives are also being endangered. He is picking up a scalpel when he shouldn't be in the operating room."

The counselor agreed that intervention should be attempted immediately. "Who are the most meaningful people in his life right now?" he asked. "Does he work with a group of physicians?" The counselor was sure from the severity of the symptoms that the other members of any such group would be aware that there was a "problem" and could be enlisted to help. But he learned from the son that —typically—the father had left the group in a huff for private practice two years before.

"Are there any brothers or sisters?"

"Yes," the clergyman said, "but all of them are now totally estranged from Father. Each one, as he or she has tried to "help," has been completely rebuffed." Family members left were the wife, a sixteen-year-old daughter, another son, twenty, and himself.

*In a recent year, over 40 percent of the patients in these hospitals were referred to the treatment units by psychiatrists who agreed with this conclusion.

"Would these four people be willing to make lists of specific behaviors by the father that had caused them concern about his drinking during the last years?" The young clergyman agreed that this would be no problem at all. "Each of us could make long lists of incidents."

The counselor then asked the young man if he thought they would be willing to read in turn these lists to the father at a meeting called for just that purpose. The young man shook his head vigorously, "No way! My sister loves Dad, but more than that she's afraid of him by now. Nowadays, he gets pretty angry when crossed. My brother would be fearful that his college career would be interrupted, financially. My mother has been threatened with divorce so frequently, she would be sure that this would bring it about. She doesn't want that. I think I'd be the only one who would be willing!"

Despite this assessment, the counselor met with the family and explained the progressive nature of the illness. He stressed the fact that by doing nothing they were actually contributing to an inevitable result. He explained to them the kinds of data, or evidence, that should be gathered and listed.

"These facts must be about *specific* incidents," he told them. "Moreover, they must be presented at the meeting in a truly nonjudgmental fashion." He emphasized that the tone of that meeting must be one of deep concern. They accepted the necessity of an attempt to intervene, and a date was chosen. They picked the early afternoon since the father was more likely to be sober.

The meeting was called at the doctor's office in a building he owned. It was his afternoon off, and he was alone. The young clergyman came directly to the point: "Actually, we are here to talk to you, Dad, about our deep concern with what is happening. Since it is no doubt going to painful, I'm going to start out by asking you to *promise,* please, to hear us out."

The father was furious. His eyes were blazing. He leapt to his feet and paced the floor. "If you think I'm going to listen to all that again, you've got another think coming!" It was a tirade.

Gently, throughout the demonstration, the son persisted, "Sit down, Dad, sit down, *please!*" Finally the father sat down and fairly shouted, "All right! I know what you're going to say, but go ahead and say it if it'll make you feel any better!"

The daughter reached into her pocket, pulled out a written list, and began timorously and fearfully, "Dad, I came home from school last Thursday with two girl friends. We came in the front door making so much noise that we woke you up on the couch. You swore at my friends so, Dad, that I'm ashamed ever to bring them over again, but I think you were so drunk that you can't remember that!"

This enraged him. He jumped to his feet and put his face six inches from hers. "After all I have done for you," he shouted, "you dare talk to me like that!" The daughter burst into tears.

The young clergyman intervened, "Dad, Dad, please hear us out! *Please!*" Finally he quieted his father and asked his sister to continue. She went on with more such events, just as specific as the first, while he pretended not to listen.

Finally he had to drop that pretense and started pushing her along. "That's twenty," he would interrupt her, as she started a new incident. "What's twenty-one?" This crazy game went on. Finally she was through.

The twenty-year-old son was next, and in a voice that trembled a bit he began quietly, "Dad, I know what you probably will do to me, but gosh, I've been worried to death, so I've got to tell it like it is. I'm your janitor in this building, and I cleaned it thoroughly three weeks ago. A week later I found five empty Scotch bottles in the places I had cleaned the week before. You're drinking on the job, Dad!" The father wiped him out with a glare, but remained silent. The young man continued through the descriptions of four or five equally specific incidents that had caused him concern.

When he finished the father's tone was menacing, "I'll take care of you, all right!"

The wife was next, and she was so fearful of his reaction that she apologized at length for what she was about to do. "I suppose this is the end of us, but then I'm convinced it would be anyway." But she plunged in. "What really got me scared happened two weeks ago," she said, and then related the story of a summons he had received on a charge of assault with a deadly weapon. "He has a gun permit because of the narcotics in his bag. And in a drunken moment, he waved his pistol in the wrong face and is being sued."

At that point, the other three in the room all exclaimed, "Mom, we didn't know that! When did that happen?" She turned to the two of her children who had already spoken and said, "I didn't know most of the things you just told about either."*

*It is important to call attention to a pattern that is typical of virtually every alcoholic situation at home or work. As the chemically dependent person moves into

She continued with her list, and a few episodes later the father jumped to his feet and dashed from the room. The family sat in stunned silence. While they were wondering what to do next, back he came carrying a case of scotch whiskey which he put at his wife's feet, exclaiming heatedly, "Okay! Okay! I get the point! You take that and get rid of it. I quit drinking!"

She was greatly relieved and obviously ready to stop, but the older son sat his father down gently, over loud protestations and urged his mother on. Bewildered, she continued, and a few minutes later the father jumped up and disappeared again. This time he returned with four partly filled bottles, obviously from various hiding places. Again he placed them at his wife's feet.

"You take those too. Now I do quit!"

She waited until he had sat down again and went on reading from her list. She came to one of the last items. "Last Tuesday," she said, "there was an emergency phone call for you. I had to say the doctor was out (and you were, too—on the couch). There was no way you could have answered that emergency, being as heavily under the influence as you were."

During the recounting of this incident, his whole demeanor changed. All the belligerence just melted away. His hands went over his face, with his elbows on his knees. It was clear that he was quietly crying.

"The patient died," his wife went on, "and I know what that cost you. I know your devotion to your patients over the last twenty-five years. I know your commitment to the Hippocratic oath. I know what that cost you." And she was finished.

The doctor went on quietly crying, but all of a sudden something hit him as he realized there was still one person in the room left to speak. This was almost the most poignant moment of all. He lowered his hands and looked at his clergyman son and shook his head as if to say, "You don't have to say anything." The respect and love they had for each other was apparent during this silent interchange.

---

his bizarre or destructive behavior, many individuals witness the behavior. They tend not to share this information with the others involved because they think it would only hurt them, or because they have some kind of misplaced loyalty to the sick person. The result, in either case, supports the sickness. They are inadvertent "enablers" of the developing condition, by their silence allowing it, to go to tragic lengths before intervention is attempted. The son who confronted his surgeon father made this clear when he said, "If I had known even half of what I've heard so far, I couldn't have waited so long to do this!"

The son nodded back at him then broke the silence gently, "Yes, I do, Dad. I'm the one who arranged this afternoon. I want to begin by saying no one could have had a better father in his boyhood and his youth. Why, just think of the days we've spent hunting together since I was big enough to carry a gun. It's been great! But last fall when you picked me up to go to the farm to hunt, you were scarcely out of town before you pulled over to the side of the road and got out to look in the trunk. You said you were checking your guns. A few miles further, the same procedure to see if we had brought the shells. Then it was to see if there was air in the spare tire. You were so drunk from the bottle in the trunk by the time we got there, I didn't go into the field with you! You were trying to put three shells in a double-barrelled shotgun!"

Loud racking sobs came from the father. The son started crying too. After they subsided, the son continued with another incident and the crying burst out again. A few episodes later, the son was finished. After some minutes the crying stopped and the father's hands came slowly down. He looked at each of his family members in turn and in a quiet, anguished voice said, "My God, I didn't know I had hurt so many people so much!"* It was the moment of reality. What he had not been able to see by himself had been made available to him in a *receivable* fashion. People cared enough to take the risk to describe his life to him in ways he could not possibly know, in order to bring him back to reality.

The room was filled with relief, and in the following hour it was mutually agreed that this was advanced alcoholism. Now the father was speaking in a reasonable and low voice. "I just can't believe that I could have done these things. I'm truly sorry!"

The clergyman son turned to what had to be done. "Dad, you're going to need help. This disease being what it is, nobody can stop drinking just by deciding to do it. I know you want to stop. There's no question in my mind about that any more."

The father was startled. "Son, do you mean that you expect me to go into a treatment setting? Why, I can't do that. That would be like my putting a sign on my building: THE DOCTOR WHO WORKS HERE IS A DRUNK. I'd lose my practice overnight. I've *got* to do this alone!"

The son was persistent. "I can see why you should be fearful, Dad.

*Contrast this with, "All right I know what you're going to say—go ahead and say it if it'll make you feel any better."

But your life is at stake. You must accept help." And the discussion continued with each remaining unmoved in his position. Finally the son offered a compromise. "Okay, Dad, let's try it your way, but let's also leave room for mine if it should become necessary. Let's agree that you make the try by yourself. Let's hope and even expect that you make it. Okay?"

"That's the way it's going to be!" the father interrupted fervently and sincerely, "You'll see!"

"Okay, but what if—just what if you can't, and you *do* drink again? What will you be willing to do?"

"Why, I'll go anywhere you say, son, if I take another drink," said the doctor, much relieved now and feeling thoroughly understood.

"No, Dad, I'd feel better if *you* told us where you would go. You know these places better than I do. You've used them for your patients."

"All right," said the father, certain that he would never have to do it because he was, in fact, through drinking. "I'll go to that hospital across town that I know has done good work in this field."

"Fair enough! That solves both our problems. But please remember, if I have to I'll hold you to your decision."

It turned out that the father did drink again, and confronted with his promise, did accept treatment in a hospital he helped to choose on the basis of its success with his patients. (Incidentally, his practice did not suffer. A year after treatment he ruefully described himself by saying, "My *new* problem is work addiction!")

Our basic assumption is that even at his sickest, the chemically dependent person can accept reality *if it is presented to him in a receivable form.* The confrontation with the surgeon illustrates the basic principles of intervention. The rules for conducting this sort of scene can be simply stated.

1. Meaningful persons must present the facts or data. That is, they must be people who do exert real influence upon the sick person. His forms of denial can and will sweep aside the efforts of others. The meaningful persons may be members of the family, as in this case, although such members will almost always need help in gaining sufficient emotional stabilization to carry out the task. The interveners may be professionals, such as physicians or clergymen, *if* they personally possess information which is useful. This would include descriptions of physical complications or behavioral patterns indicating the presence of the disease.

The most effective interveners, however, because they are the most meaningful of all, are employers or the members of management at the level next above the chemically dependent person. Individuals tend to put their own greatest value as people on their productivity, so the boss is the most meaningful person.*

In any case, for the most part intervention should not be attempted alone, although it can be done. Groups of at least two or three seem most effective. They tend to support each other in getting the task accomplished successfully, and also have the necessary weight to break through to reality.

2. The data presented should be specific and descriptive of events *which have happened* or conditions *which exist.* "I was there when you insulted our client, and it was obvious to both the client and to me that you'd had too many," or "The word around the office is not to send you clients after lunch. The others often feel you aren't in shape to take care of them." Obviously evidence is strongest when it is firsthand.

Opinions are to be avoided, along with all generalizations. "I think you have been drinking too much," or "I think you ought to quit drinking entirely," are worse than useless. All such general opinions do is to raise the defenses still higher and make the approach to reality more difficult.

3. The tone of the confrontation should not be judgmental. The data should show concern; in truth, the facts are simply items to demonstrate the legitimacy of the concern being expressed. "I am really worried about what has been happening to you, and these are the facts available to me which will give you the reasons why I am so concerned." The list of facts follows.

4. The chief evidence should be tied directly into drinking wherever possible. "After the company picnic last Saturday, I saw you leave a bit under the weather. I assumed that your wife would do the driving, but I learned that you drove nearly 100 mph on the freeway with your family in the car." The more general data should only be used to support the examples of drinking. "Your production has gone down this year."

5. The evidence of behavior should be presented in some detail, to

*A refrain among hospitalized male patients is, "At least I didn't drink on the job." In fact, a rule of thumb seems to be that when drinking does appear at work, one can assume a late stage of the illness. It is very likely that a multitude of problems are already present elsewhere.

give the sick person a panoramic view of himself during a given period of time. He himself does not and cannot have this view because of his deluded condition. He is out of touch with reality. His greatest need is to be confronted by it. Sound movies or tapes of some of his drinking episodes will do it best. No argument is possible, no denial can be made. There he is on the silver screen or on tape, acting and sounding like that. ("My God, I didn't know I had hurt so many people so much!") The interveners are to act for the silver screen. "This is reality! Reality *is not what you have been believing* it was!"

6. The goal of the intervention, through the presentation of this material, is to have him see and accept enough reality so that, however grudgingly, he can accept in turn his need for help.

7. At this point, the available choices acceptable to the interveners may be offered. And in many sections of the country there are choices. The key person confronting the alcoholic may say, "Since abstinence is a basic requirement, these alternatives are before us: *this* treatment center, *that* hospital, or AA. Which help will you use?" Allowing him, in some way, to be a part of the decision-making is to offer him some sense of dignity, which is obviously important. Firmness here, however, is again necessary. His defenses can and very likely will regroup quickly unless he is sure the interveners mean what they say.

Under the first principle of intervention, we said that an executive of the next rank up, or the boss, is likely to be the most meaningful person. The boss may be the last to know that his employee is alcoholic; on the other hand, he may be the first person to do something about it. He is not as entangled as members of the immediate family, and does not suffer the effects of the disease as they do. Since the Johnson Institute has industrial and business clients, we work with a great many executives, and they frequently set up appointments for their key employees. So the boss instead of a member of the immediate family may set up the confrontation.

One of the top executives of a company we are working with called us about one of their key employees who had "a four-year history of psychiatric care." He went on to tell about "nervous exhaustion episodes" and all sorts of other interruptions of his productive work. He said that what he had learned from the program on alcoholism made him suspicious that this might be the problem. So we advised that the next time there was an incident of absenteeism, he should suggest that the man come in to us.

He did come in. And did reveal that he had been going to a

psychiatrist, that he had had nervous problems. But we could get at no data that were useful to us. We presented the Feeling Chart to him. He said it was very interesting, that it applied to a couple of people he knew, but certainly didn't fit him. What we were picking up from him empathetically, however, made us sure that he had an alcoholic problem; yet there was no way it could be nailed down. So we reported this to his superior. We told him that one of the difficulties we had with this sort of approach was that an alcoholic's defense systems were so rigid that they often could not be penetrated in a one-to-one situation, and explained that it would be necessary to get a member of his immediate family to give us firsthand information about him. We then agreed that after the next episode—knowing there would be one—we would bring the wife in.

A month later there was an incident. His superior arranged for the wife to come in and for her to bring along their two sons, eighteen and twenty-six, for a family discussion of the company's problem with this employee. It was a very tense group. The father was a well-dressed, well-groomed, well-organized man in his late forties or early fifties. He was impressive, but not entirely normal-looking—his anxiety showed. The boss introduced the counselor to the wife, and it was apparent that she was terribly anxious and cautious. The superior started out by saying, "I have asked for this interview because I'm convinced we need professional help to get at every possibility that might be involved here. Our concern as a company is that we have a four-year history of absenteeism with a variety of nervous disorders. We are afraid that we may be putting too much on you, Bill. Maybe we should reorganize the work so that you don't have the load you apparently have. We are worried about the company's responsibility to you as a human being."

He went on to say that the company had adopted a new policy on employees with chemical problems, and that they were not separated for this reason. Then he turned to the wife and said, "I would like to have the counselor explain just what the Johnson Institute does do with us." So the counselor opened it up by saying, "Bill, you remember our conversation in my office. I pointed out to you that a man cannot give accurate information about his own chemical problem. The illness prevents it. So today there is no way I can ask you direct questions and you can give me direct answers that will help me to make a diagnosis."

The counselor sympathized with the wife in her uncomfortable position and said, "I sense that you may feel you're playing Judas to your husband, but I need certain facts from you." Then he asked her, "Does he drink? I have asked him and he says, 'Some.' Do you think it is more than 'some'?"

"I drink too. He probably drinks more than I do, I guess, sometimes."

"I understand your reticence. Has he been drunk in the last month?"

"Well, what do you mean 'drunk'?"

"I mean drunk—most people know what I mean when I say that. I mean showing signs of intoxication: slurred words, weaving gait, or . . ."

"We-e-ell, yes. Once or twice." It's like pulling teeth.

Finally her reaction is silence. And all this silence is telling the counselor, *boy, have I hit a responsive chord!* So he kept repeating to her, "I understand, I understand, you feel you might say some things now that your husband will never forgive you for. I know you are too fearful." At this point she turned to her eldest son and said, "You know I can't talk about Dad like that."

And he said, "Mom, I can. I can talk. I've been worried sick. I've been alternately angry and furious and worried for years." And he turned to his father and said, "Dad I'm going to tell it like it is. Dad, last week you were gone for three days from work—Monday and Tuesday and Wednesday. It started over the weekend, and you didn't come out of the bedroom except to get another bottle."

The father made some pretty threatening statements in the course of the next ten minutes. Quietly threatening, but threatening. Like "You haven't been around the house," and "If you had to put up with what I have to put up with . . . You ought to understand at your age." And "You've been siding with your mother all these years."

The son said, "And more than that, when we took all the booze out of that house last week, you got up and dressed and went out and bought more. And you had no business driving in your condition."

The mother was asked about the experience that had brought her husband into the Johnson Institute in the first place, and she finally opened up: "Well, that was another great big drunk, he was laid up for five days. He's a binge drinker."

Then the superior put in: "Now, there is more than just smoke around you. I knew there was some fire in these events." And he described how as an executive representing the company the man had made a speech in a downtown hotel. He had been visibly intoxicated in the podium. The explanation had been that he was so fumbling and bumbling in his presentation because he was ultranervous. "That wasn't nerves," the boss said. "The people around you knew it was drink, even though the general public may not have."

Then the counselor confronted the executive with a review of the situation and emphasized his boss's concern. "Chuck, here, was worried sick about you, and he reminded me that you'd been a valuable employee for twenty-five years. Everybody wants to help," the counselor said. "What are you willing to do?"

"Well, I'll quit drinking."

"Oh, you've said that a dozen times," his wife said.

"Well, I will this time."

Then the counselor, after appraising the situation, reiterated that this deep into the pattern, with the binges getting closer together, it was a very serious matter. "They used to be six months apart, and now they're three weeks apart—you haven't got a chance of doing this without help. My suggestion is that you go for treatment." At this point, the supervisor broke in, "That was made as a suggestion, but I've got to insist on it for the company's sake now. We can't take any half measures. We have to go all the way on this."

"Well, I just spent three weeks in a psychiatric ward and I'm not going to another hospital. You should have seen the . . ." He expressed the fear he had felt in this locked ward. The counselor heard him out. Then he explained how this treatment was different and told him in detail about the hospitals he could choose from. He described St. Mary's Hospital, where "all the doors open out," and Hazelden, which was "physically like a very fine, plush, brand-new motel." Finally he recommended St. Mary's because of its proximity to the family.

Then the counselor turned to the wife. "The thing I've noticed immediately about you," he said, "is that you've become so distressed in living with this disease that you're practically immobilized." She burst into tears. Somebody understood her. She was crying with relief. She said, "God, if somebody would only help me." The counselor said, "Help is here. I'm recommending a place that will provide help for both of you."

Now, in this sort of confrontation it is almost impossible to secure and maintain the data flow from these two people. He is so far advanced into his illness that he cannot answer the question, "Do you drink?" by anything more than "occasionally." And when she is confronted with his sort of behavior, she cannot come forward and give an account of it. All she can do is to be immobilized by it. Only because the two sons are relatively uninvolved emotionally are they able to describe what has been happening.

Incidentally, that man did come to St. Mary's Hospital. He went back to Chicago about eighteen months ago, and he had responded beautifully to treatment. He is so grateful to the company that he has written on several occasions to express that gratitude, and his willingness to appear publicly before any group on any occasion that would be useful.

6.

The Cry for Help and the Use of Crisis

"What the hell do you expect me to do?"

The confrontations of the surgeon and the businessman were carefully set up and rehearsed. All the rules of confrontation were employed, with the most meaningful people available gathered together, and the data or facts about the drinking episodes were specific and based on firsthand information. Yet both victims were extremely difficult to reach. Reality was presented to them, and finally accepted after a real struggle. Confrontation is not always so difficult, and it may take place by itself, in the most surprising ways.

The shortest intervention I ever made in my life *happened* to me about four o'clock one Friday afternoon, when I was sitting in my office at the Johnson Institute alone. This fellow barged right past my secretary, and he stood there and began to cuss me out in Anglo-Saxon that even I was still learning. He said, "I want you to know I'm gonna sue you for every dime you've got. I don't suppose you've got much, but I'm gonna take everything you have. Then, I'm gonna close this goddamn place!"

My secretary was ready to call the police. I hadn't said "Hi," "Yes," "No," "Sit down," or anything. I had never laid eyes on him before. And he started out by saying, "Now, you've alienated my wife and her affections." And then he said, "I'm Joe Smith." And I said, "Oh yes, Mrs. Smith." She had been in two or three times, and I had been instructing her how to intervene in her husband's illness. I didn't say anything more. I knew he was the husband I had been hearing about.

So he said, "One of the things I want you to know is that I'm not alcoholic—that's defamation of character and I'm going to get you for that. So I got you for alienation and I got you for defamation. There is no way I could be an alcoholic." And he went on as to why. "I've had plenty of opportunities to be alcoholic, married to that blanky, blanky, blank blank." This led to a fifteen-minute tirade against his wife. Then he said, "If you think I'm going to go to Hazelden, and I haven't even met you, you don't know a thing about me." And then he went on about his job. All the pressures of it, and without him the whole company would have folded up. And there wasn't anybody around there who gave him any credit. Another fifteen minutes.

He continued, "And I want you to know that just because of that blanky, blank, blank job, I couldn't possibly spend three weeks in any kind of treatment center like Hazelden." (That just dropped in there.) "And besides," he said, "I've been losing money," and then he went on about his wife spending money, money, money, and all his problems with money—another ten minutes. Then he said, "So I haven't even got the six hundred it takes to go to Hazelden."

Now already I'd had three clues in the hour he'd been talking: "If you think I'm going to Hazelden," "I couldn't possibly spend three weeks in Hazelden," and "I don't have the money to go to Hazelden." When the third one came, I still hadn't said a word. I reached over, took the phone off the hook and poised my finger over it. I said, "Joe, I'm going to call Hazelden and make an appointment for you. When could you go?"

He glared at me, spitting fire. "Not before tomorrow morning."

He went, and he's living in St. Louis now. He has been sober ever since.

Not only is this the shortest intervention I have ever had, but it beautifully illustrates the *cry for help.* Unconsciously, this tirade was a desperate plea for assistance. He wouldn't come into my office and threaten me if he were going to take legal action against me, and I knew from what he said that I had no reason to fear him. He was a big guy; if he had wanted to, he would have attacked me when he first came in.

The cry for help can go unheard or completely misunderstood by the spouse or any other involved person who does not know how to listen for it. In an incident that happened some years ago, there is a good example of a clear cry for help which an exhausted, desperate spouse completely failed to pick up. I had just reached home at nine-thirty one night—after a fourteen-hour day. The phone rang and a fellow down in the suburb where I live said, "My daughters and I have confronted my wife. We've been at it for four hours and we're at an impasse. Vernon, can you come over and help us?"

"Fourteen hours I've been at it—just to tell you where I am—I couldn't be any use to you. I've had it! Now, can you—this problem has been ten years coming—drop what you're doing right now at this moment? Bundle your wife into the car in the morning and be at my office at eight o'clock. Whatever I'm doing I'll cancel."

He said, "I understand, Vernon, and I'll see that we're there in the morning . . ." Now, she had overheard what he was saying, I could hear her voice in the background: "If that's all either one of you cares about me, the hell with both of you!"

So I said, "George, *that's the mating call of a suffering alcoholic.* I'll be right over." And I jumped in my car; I was all enthused again. When I heard that, I felt sure it would be an easy time. Sure enough, forty-five minutes later we were putting her into a car and she was off for St. Mary's Hospital. As I went out the door—her husband was going to take her down—I put out my hand and said, "Doris, I want to tell you something right now. I mean it from the bottom of my heart. I think you've made the greatest decision you could possibly have made in your whole lifetime. This will change your life from this day forward and it's all for the better." She collapsed around my neck, and with her head on the side away from her husband, said into my ear, "Thank God, somebody did something!"

He himself was utterly astonished at the way things had gone, every second of that confrontation had seemed to him absolutely fruitless. To begin with, he could not understand why I had changed my mind—could not hear the cry for help that I heard. When she said, "If that's all either one of you cares. . . ." I knew the translation was, "Please help me!" When the alcoholic says, "Well what the hell do you expect me to do?" it means "What are you going to ask me to do?" This is called *defiant dependence.* The defiance is caused by all the massive emotional distress, and the dependence is revealed by, "What do you expect me to do?" A reaching out, saying, "Okay, here I am. How come you didn't do something like this before?"

Whether or not you are able to hear a cry for help, it's there, and intervention is absolutely necessary. The real reason we intervene is that spontaneous insight is impossible. Let us consider the alternate route. So you wait until the alcoholic bottoms out. You haven't taken any risks. He is not dangerous to approach; you don't create a terrible scene; you are not going to break up a friendship; you are not going to separate yourself from your child or your mate. It may be easier to accomplish, but by this time all that is left to do is to put a pine box around him. We believe in intervention because a person's life is in danger. It is as necessary as surgery when peritonitis is inevitable. The chief misconception is that spontaneous insight may occur. When you examine the lives of those who claim to have had it, you discover that a buildup of crises has forced them to look at the reality of their condition. The only way back to reality is through crisis.

Yet today when an alcoholic gets into trouble the typical response is to try to minimize it. "Let's hush this up. Let's see if we can't keep it out of the paper. Let's see if we can't get a lawyer to get the judge to reduce the charge." There are all sorts of ways of minimizing the force and the pain of each crisis as it develops. While we are trying to be helpful, we are actually aiding and abetting the development of the disease. Every time you try to rescue an alcoholic, you are delaying useful treatment.

Crises did not have to be invented or created around the surgeon—he had one every day. It was an accumulation of crises that drove his desperate son, the clergyman, to seek help. Crises are opportunities—they need not be terrifying. The problem is to get people knowledgeable enough to use them creatively. For instance, the Johnson Institute urges that the laws against drunken driving be enforced—to create crises. Out of crises come the opportunities for intervention. The resulting confrontations can break through to reality as the first step back toward health. This is the beginning of treatment.

It will be the task of treatment to make the alcoholic well. It is the task of intervention to bring him to treatment.

7.

Treatment of the Acute Phase

"All he has to do is quit drinking"

By now the reader will understand what an ironic misconception this is—how far this popular assessment is from any understanding of the dynamics of alcoholism. Abstinence is not the only goal of therapy; the real purpose is the restoration of adequate ego strength to enable the victim once again to cope with life situations.

Therapy for the alcoholic must treat the whole man. He suffers emotionally, mentally, physically, and spiritually. Our program came to be designed with this whole spectrum in mind. Our interdisciplinary team includes physicians, clergymen, psychologists, sociologists, pathologists, and psychiatrists, as well as the regular personnel of a hospital setting. This means that nurses, administrative people, orderlies, janitors, everybody is involved. (See Appendix H.) In the hospitals that use this system, everyone is part of the treatment team.*

If the whole man is not treated simultaneously, relapse is inevitable. If the emotional disorder alone is reduced, the patient leaves medical care thinking he "can handle it," now that he feels so well. Then his experimentation with alcohol wipes out the gains made in his emotional environment and sends him plunging back down the same old self-destructive spiral. (See Appendix A.)

*Just the matter of sympathy comes to mind. Nurses are trained to be sympathetic to pain in other sections of the hospital. Here such a response is almost never useful and is often detrimental to the progress of the treatment. When a patient has been thoroughly and directly confronted in "group" in an effort to present him with reality, he may seek sympathy. He reports *his* version to the untrained nurse, who is shocked and replies, "You poor fellow! I don't blame you one bit for being angry with them." His defenses are supported. She learns with training to listen to the story and say, "Yes, I understand how you feel. Everybody feels that way during the first few days, and like the others, I'm sure you'll soon come to see what they're driving at. Meantime, chin up, my friend."

Or if only the mental mismanagement is brought under control (awareness and acceptance of the logical reasons for abstinence), the emotional burdens continue in force. The patient remains easily irritated, anxious, nervous, or depressed. The mass of free-floating negative feelings is still present, bringing on waves of self-pity and resentment. He overreacts to simple frustrations; he is judgmental, omnipotent, hypersensitive, critical, tense, and unpredictable. In fact, his family reports, "He was easier to live with when he was drinking."

The symptoms of the "dry drunk" are most evident and damaging to family and others immediately around the sick person. As one spouse put it, "It doesn't matter whether you're sober or not, you just aren't the same person I married." One dry alcoholic came out of the "dry" experience with a startling insight. "Now I see," he said, "that when I went on the wagon those times, all I did was go on a series of dry drunks."

As this condition worsens, his mental gains erode away and he inevitably reverts to drinking "to feel normal." The great lesson of his past takes over, "It moves me in the right direction, and it works *every time.* Just one to get over the hump!" Rationalizations resume their old place in his life, and back he plunges. The characterological conflict continues to grow, and the drinking with it.

Both of these conditions—mental and emotional—must be reduced while his physical needs are receiving medical attention if he is to be stabilized into a chemically free life-style.

Our interdisciplinary design for treatment can best be understood by following the experience of a typical patient as he comes to a hospital after the kind of confrontation scene described in the preceding chapter. He is beginning a minimum of three weeks of intensive care for the acute symptoms of his disease. (See Appendixes C, D, and E.)

He goes through admission and detoxification, if needed, and spends twenty-four hours under observation. He is in bed, with a medical regime for withdrawal and a routine medical checkup. Contrary to popular belief, physical withdrawal usually presents no major problems and can be handled simply with good medical management.

After this initial period, our man is placed in a room and assigned to a counselor. Immediately he begins attending the lectures that make up the mental management phase of treatment. Their purpose is to bring him to an intellectual understanding of the *primary nature* of the chemical dependency syndrome. It is the harmful dependency itself that has resulted in the self-destructive or other destructive behaviors.

During these three weeks, he will attend approximately sixty lectures given by members of the hospital staff and visiting professionals from the community. Factual information will be presented from many different disciplines. Old wives' tales must be replaced by accurate and scientific information presented in such a way that he can comprehend and accept it.

"Alcohol is a *depressant;* not what you have up to now thought it to be. And here is how it acts." Not only are the effects on the brain explained to him by the physician in a series of talks, but the progressive effects on all vital organs of the body are carefully detailed. The emotional syndrome receives equal attention in lectures by the psychiatrist, psychologist, or other trained person. The operations of psychological defense systems are detailed, and how they can, and in this disease *do* bring people temporarily out of touch with reality. The characteristics of anxious people, the dynamics of interpersonal relationships, and the emotional effects of desocialization are given specific attention.

Others, including clergymen and social workers, lecture on value systems. They elaborate on the emotional effects of behavior which is repeatedly in contradiction to those values, and the destructiveness of chronic feelings of guilt, shame, or remorse on individuals victimized by compulsive behavior. They develop examples of the ways such conflicts are resolved. Spiritual impoverishment is described with cause, effect, and resolutions made clear. Problems in communication are stressed, and more useful ways to gain much needed skills in this area are discussed.

The tenets of Alcoholics Anonymous are presented, and an introduction to each of the "Twelve Suggested Steps of Recovery" is given by lecturers who are themselves members of AA. (Patients are told, by living example, that recovery is possible.)

These and many other related subjects are presented in the three-week cycle of lectures. They are accompanied by appropriate films or slides, and are reinforced by books and pamphlets as assigned reading.

The primary goal of this didactic effort is to help the patient realize intellectually that chemical dependency is a disease entity capable of accurate description in each of its several manifestations, and to convince him that these descriptions apply across the board to all who suffer from the disease.*

Consequently, he can make an intellectual identification of his own condition as being *that disease*—with two very significant results:

First, he makes a mental commitment to cooperate in his treatment and to adopt a measure of responsibility for his own recovery.

The other significant result has to do with changing the patient's initial attitude. When he arrives for treatment he thinks he is alone in his condition. His situation is unique. He has sensed himself as isolated, abandoned, or deserted; has felt *apart,* yet paradoxically has had a strong need to conceal the fact that he feels so separated from others. Now he learns that there are other people—and many of them—who are in the same boat. The very concept of his problem being a disease attacks his consuming sense of loneliness. By consciously attaching himself to his fellow sufferers, he starts his resocialization process.† He is beginning, as he puts it, "to rejoin the human race."

While attending these lectures, our man is an ambulatory patient in a section of the hospital designed specifically for him and other victims of the same illness; he is in constant contact with the other chemically dependent patients. Thus exchange is made possible and socializing encouraged. The patients walk to the cafeteria together for meals, share coffee breaks, sports activities, and clean-up chores. Each person is assigned to a group of seven or eight with whom he meets every day for at least two hours in a therapy session. This group life is led by a trained counselor and is designed to accomplish two specific goals.

As stated in the *Patients' Handbook* (see Appendix A), these goals are:

> To discover ourselves and others as feeling persons, and
>
> To identify the defenses that prevent this discovery.

In these sessions the second goal comes first, and the primary task of the group is to identify the patient's defenses and describe them to him in such ways as will give him an opportunity to recognize them. Later on, in the group, he will learn that it is these highly developed

*A frequent remark by the patients is, "Thank God they've told me what's wrong with me! This is bad, but I thought I was going crazy!"

†Our lecturers frequently have patients come up to them at the end, smiling and saying, "Hey, you've been reading my mail again. This is weird! How can you know me so well?" The smile indicates some of the relief that comes from "belonging" again.

and rigid defenses that keep the free-floating mass of negative attitudes and feelings locked up. He will come to understand that the locked-up feelings, in turn, bind him into his stereotyped self-destructive pattern of life. Notice, the defenses are called to his attention and named *while he is actually employing them.* The chances of recognition are thus greatly enhanced. An illustration is useful perhaps.

Figure XII

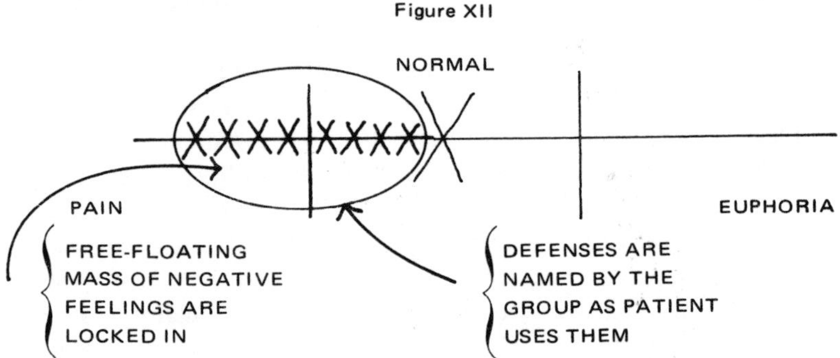

Our man in the graph came to his first group meeting alert and very much on guard. Although his anxiety was running high, outwardly he appeared calm (a little red in the ears, maybe), and he listened attentively to the goings-on of the first few minutes. Then another, more experienced patient turned to him and said, "Hi Joe! We met last night. I'm glad you're in this group. Say, we're going to be living together like this for some weeks, and it certainly would help to know you better. Do you mind telling us a little about yourself?" Joe smiled a bit cautiously but nodded his head.

"Sure thing! My name's Joe. I'm married and we have three children, ages from fifteen to nineteen. I live out by the lake west of town in a nice, typical suburb. And oh yes, I'm a broker. I guess you know what that is. I sell stocks and bonds. Probably I should say that I've been *trying* to sell them. What's happened to the market these last eighteen months has made it almost impossible." And he went on about the falling market conditions.

Finally the other patient interrupted with, "Yeah, I guess there's been a problem with the market, all right. But what I really meant to ask was, how did you get *here?*"

Joe reddened perceptibly and his voice rose a bit as he said, "I've been trying to tell you, but I guess you haven't been really listening. For eighteen solid months the market's been dropping. Old customers have been on my back like you can't believe! 'Buy me something that *makes* money, not *loses* it,' is all I've heard. You can't imagine the pressure I've been under!" and he paused, looking as though he had answered the question.

The other patient picked it up, "Yeah, I get it. I get it. The pressure. Knowing what I know about the market I'm sure you had pressure. But how come you got *here?*" he persisted quietly.

"Doggone it, I've already told you! It was the pressure. Bigger brokerage houses than ours have gone down the drain. And I guess it got to me some. I got to drinking a little . . . sometimes . . . maybe!"

"Joe, do you know what you've been doing these last fifteen minutes?" the other patient asked.

"I've been trying to explain to you how I got here. You asked me . . ." Joe's voice was sharp.

"Oh, you've been explaining all right, and that's exactly the point. What you've been doing these last fifteen minutes, Joe, is trying to tell all of us in this room that you believe there's a legitimate reason for drinking yourself to death! Around here we have a name for that. It's called "rationalizing," Joe. And that kind of rationalizing is just what is going to keep you drinking yourself into the grave. Why, you sound like you actually believe business pressure's a legitimate reason for the way you've been hitting the bottle!"

Joe glared in silence. Another patient picked it up. "Let me tell you another one of your defenses, Joe. It's called "minimizing." You said you got to drinking a *little, sometimes, maybe.* Why, you were two extra days in detox when you were admitted here this week!* Nobody gets that sick on drinking a little, sometimes, maybe!"

So it went on through the two hours, and Joe left the room that day certain of at least two things. "No one in that room understood me for one minute," he said to himself. "And it's for damn sure they don't know anything about the brokerage business in 1970!"

But the poor fellow had to be back in the same room the very next morning. And now he was ready! He had spent the night going over

*The detoxification area is located right in the unit. One reason for this is that much important learning takes place with the patients as a group. The more severe withdrawal symptoms which occasionally appear are object lessons for them. Moreover, data such as these become available for use by counselors or other patients in group confrontations.

it all, and he had thought out a way of countering every maneuver they could make. He was twice as alert and wary and therefore *listening hard,* because he was sure the next sentence would be directed at him. However, the group had other matters and other people to attend to. The day came and went without anybody paying any attention to him, and the following day was the same. Joe was left to himself.

On the fourth day, another newcomer arrived in the group. Joe thought he looked like a nice enough fellow (though he seemed a little the worse for wear); he even had a familiar face. In due time one of the more experienced patients turned to him and asked, "Henry, would you mind telling us a little bit about yourself?"

Joe thought Henry looked a little nervous, but his voice sounded all right.

"Oh sure! I'm Henry. I'm married, with two kids, fourteen and sixteen. We live in the south part of town. I'm a banker by profession. One of the officers at the First here downtown, on the lending side—I'm a loan officer. And wow! Has this last eighteen months been a tough pull! You know—no money to lend—rising interest rates—" and he went on about the impossibility of his job until one of the other patients quietly interrupted. "But how come you got *here?*"

"Well, actually I've been telling you," said Henry. At that moment something popped in Joe's head. He sat on the edge of his chair and leaned forward as Henry explained. "When you've been in the banking business as long as I have, with the list of regular customers I've built up, and almost every single one of them harassing you for money that isn't there—well, you can't imagine the pressure!"

"Henry!" Joe shot it in before anyone else could speak. "Henry, what you're doing *right now,* when you're trying to build up business pressure as a valid reason for drinking yourself to death, has got a name. It's called *rationalizing.* What scares me is that I see you believe it's a valid reason for drinking like you've been drinking. I was doing exactly the same thing only four days ago in this very room—and I believed it, too!"

And the rest of the group broke into roars of laughter. "Atta boy, Joe! You're going to make it yet!"*

Notice, in this illustration, that the primary goal is strictly adhered

*This incident really took place. Only the names have been changed to protect identities.

to. No effort to *change* the patient was made. His defenses were simply called to his attention and given names. It was left to him to recognize them, and in his own time to accept them as his.

No attempt to manipulate the patient goes unnoticed. Should such an attempt be made by one patient on another, the counselor would step in and call attention to what is happening. "What's going on with you, that you think you have to *fix* him? *Fixing* is a dirty word in this group, and anyway it doesn't work. It's up to him to fix himself if he's going to get well. He's here only to get our description of how he's operating *as we see it.* It is up to him to accept or reject what we tell him about himself."

Once they had confronted Joe with his rationalization, he was left to think it out. When the second patient, Henry, used a similar defense (in this case it was an exact parallel), Joe could and then did see himself in Henry's behavior. Then he could accept his own rationalization as being out of touch with reality. The recognition scene itself effectively reduced his defenses to more manageable levels. He became more open to useful interpersonal relationships. The same reduction occurred with his projections as time went on. "It sure is a surprise to see how much my wife has improved since I got here!" Self-hatred was gradually recognized for what it was—*self*-hatred—and he saw how and why self-loathing was his problem. "Anybody behaving as I've behaved *should* hate himself!"

As these defenses were modified to more normal levels, his next therapeutic problem became available and workable. The mass of negative emotional life was gradually exposed. He sat in group one day, and one of his newfound friends confronted him abruptly, "Joe, you certainly have been tough to live with the last two days—what's going on with you?"

Joe snapped back, "What do you mean, what's going on with me?"

"Well, to tell you the truth, just like when you said that right now, you've been so touchy, so angry-looking most of the time, I've been a little afraid to talk to you. You've been pretty hostile, and it's made me uncomfortable."

"Hostile?!—who's hostile?" Joe shouted at him.

"That's what I mean, Joe—right there. What your feeling is right now is what I have been noticing the last couple of days."

Joe went to his room after group, upset and still aware of the strength of this newly exposed feeling. He tried to justify it by calling it righteous indignation, but that didn't work. He couldn't think of what he was indignant about. He kept on wrestling with it, and so did the group the next day. It was there, in group with the others, that it dawned. "I'm resentful; in fact, I'm loaded with resentments. I'm a resentful person!" He said it again and again. "That's why I've been so hostile."

The group agreed that he had discovered something important about himself, but reminded him that he didn't have to continue living with all that resentment. Then a fellow patient moved on to confront him still further. "While we're on it, Joe, I want to tell you another thing I've noticed about you. I noticed it the first day, when you were telling us how tough it is to be a broker, and during the last few days when you've been complaining about . . . (he listed four other grievances). I hear you telling us how sorry you are for yourself. Life is pretty tough for you isn't it, Joe? How do you feel right now?"

"*Will* you get off my back?" Joe said as he glared at the man confronting him.

"Joe, your resentfulness is showing again, and again it's making me pretty uncomfortable," a third member of the group said to him.

The counselor entered with, "Joe, these people are telling you some things about yourself you would do well to think about."

"*I* think about it," he snapped. "That's all I hear around here! I came here to get some help, and all I've gotten is insulted or bored to death. Lectures and groups and groups and lectures, day after day. 'Your resentfulness is showing, Joe! Your self-pity is showing, Joe!' When do I get some help? I get a pain in my stomach, and I go to the doctor and I get help. The doctor gives me something for it!"

Another quiet patient who had not entered the conversation until now shook his head and hesitantly said, "Joe, you're doing it again! Resentment and self-pity, both!"

The whole group was against him, he felt.

Joe turned to the counselor, still glaring, "All right! All right! You're the counselor here. If I'm loaded with resentment and self-pity, what are you going to do about it? You're the doctor, I'm told." His tone was defiant.

The counselor simply said, "I can't do it for you, Joe. What we can do, we're doing."

That night Joe attended a lecture on characterological conflict and the chronic negative feelings which such conflict causes. He did some hard thinking. He began to see that self-pity was strongly present inside of him, and that if it remained there as an attitude it would seriously endanger his recovery.

Notice in this illustration a number of typical patient reactions. First of all, the patient is opening up, which indicates a significant reduction of his defenses. While those defenses were rigidly intact, he could present himself with only very little affect. If described as thoroughly angry, he would have replied with a slight raising of his eyebrows but an emotionless voice, "All right, if you say so, I'm angry." In the same listless tone of voice, a little later on he would have said, "I'm happy." Neither would have been believable.

Repression is not only operating at the memory level to cause the delusion, but is also acting strongly and just as unconsciously against the growing mass of negative feelings about himself. Guilt, shame, remorse, and all the "I'm no damn good" feelings must be repressed in the interest of survival, and this repression is, therefore, a real part of the defense wall (the circle on the left side of the emotion graph —see Fig. XIII.)

Figure XIII

PHASE THREE AND FOUR:REPRESSION

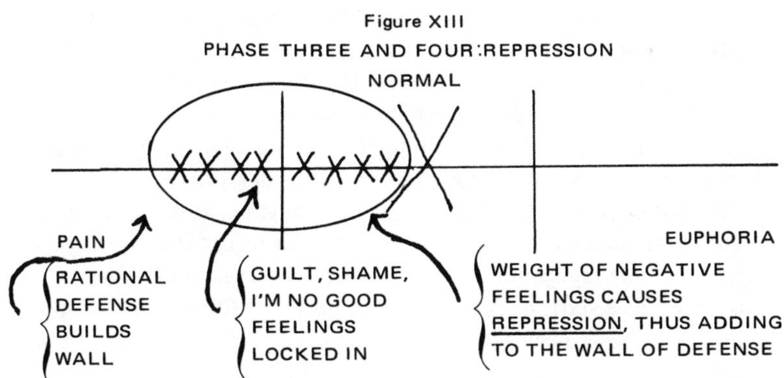

Unfortunately, repression is apparently not selective in its effects, and the baby goes out with the bath—i. e., good feelings are repressed along with the bad. Apathy, or no feeling, is the result.

It is our experience that working with the good feelings during the early stages of therapy is next to impossible. They are simply overridden or overlaid by the bad, which always appear first in therapy and must be modified before the more constructive emotions can become available at a characterological level. This fact speaks to the counselor's approach to the patient. If he is accurately empathetic with this condition, he will know the futility of approaching the chemically dependent person by cajoling or appealing to his positive side in any way. If early on, for example, he says to the patient, "You're really a good guy!" the patient, while he may smile and mutter his thanks, will be put off. He will be thinking, "Either this guy doesn't know me at all, or he doesn't know this disease, or he is after something!" He will reject both the thought and the counselor.

Far better if the counselor were to say at this early stage, "I can understand why you feel so badly about yourself after all you have done these recent years!" The patient might scowl, but inside something is saying, "He knows what pain I am going through, and maybe I can trust him after all." The relationship will grow, at the level of this "tough love," as it is called at one of the hospitals.

Another typical patient reaction at this stage of therapy is his defiant-dependent relationship to his counselor and the therapy in general. "If there is something wrong with me, *you* fix it!" is the message he is sending at this point. The manner of sending it will vary with the person, of course. In fact, it may be done so subtly that the counselor and the group may well find themselves feeling downright guilty for not helping more. In any case, defiance is real at this stage, and yet, paradoxically, a still unhealthy dependence is also present. All the counselor can do is mark it on the chart as a point of progress (for it is that) and steadfastly reply, "I'm not going to 'fix' you because I can't! What are *you* doing about meeting this problem?"

The patient is seen as progressing. He is starting, at least, to identify some components of what, up to now, has been that free-floating and therefore unrecognizable mass of negative feelings and attitudes. At this stage, as a start, he is conscious of his resentfulness and self-pity. Moreover, he is beginning to recognize them as symptoms of his emotional disorder. Again it is to be noted that the goal of the group is not to change these attitudes, but to cause the patient to become *aware* of their chronic presence.

A comment on two simple norms of the group life will indicate how these recognition scenes around feelings and attitudes take place. The first norm is that questions which probe for the current feeling life are encouraged. "How are you feeling right now, Joe?" Over and over again he will reply to that question with an intellectual evasion, such as, "I feel that you are trying to get me to say something!" He will then be told that that reply was itself an intellectual defense and an effort to avoid looking at his own feelings, and that the effect of the defense was to shift attention to the other person. "Joe, it would have

Figure XIV
THERAPY GOALS PERSONAL INSIGHT

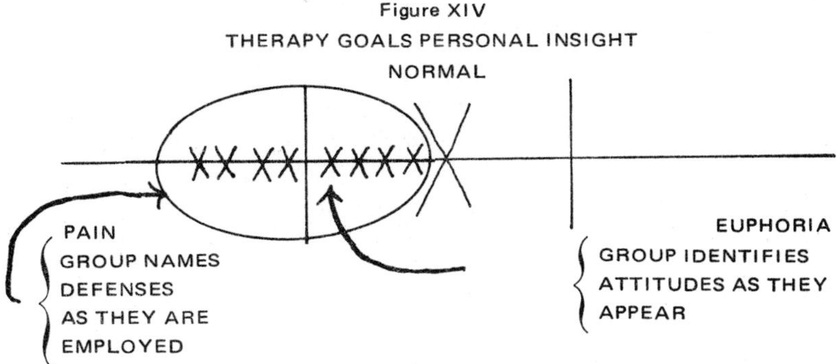

been more accurate if you had said, "I *think* (not I *feel)* that you are trying to get me to say something. It didn't tell me or you anything about your feelings. I think you are so busy right now defending yourself that you don't even know how you feel."

In that kind of interchange, two valuable confrontations are accomplished.* The continued defensiveness is revealed and described, as well as the still "locked in" condition of the feeling life.

The second norm built into the group is that questions beginning with *why* are conscientiously to be avoided. "Why did you say that, Joe?" may be asked perfectly innocently, in the belief that it will cause Joe to look at his feelings and report them, with a "because I am anxious and even a little fearful." The effect, however, is to force him into further intellectualizations: "Because, I believe you are trying to get me to say something!" Given the goal of reducing rational defenses, the *why* questions are self-defeating. They push the patient from the emotional to the entirely rational response.†

*Confrontations are often mistaken as being forms of attacking the individual. Attacking, obviously, serves only to raise defenses, and if employed at all should be used only and deliberately to make defenses more apparent. Confrontation, on the other hand, is defined as a *description* of the other person, made in such a way as is most likely to be receivable by him.

†Another reason *why* questions are avoided is that they force the group life into another and unwanted model. It becomes a problem-solving group. Sentences like this start arriving, "When that happened at my house, I'll tell you what *I* did about it!" The wise counselor brings that to a halt with, "So that's how you got here! Let's get back to the business at hand!" (See *Group Therapy Handbook,* Appendix B.)

The data to be employed in confrontation of the patient are most useful when they are from the group life itself. They carry the weight of personal experience with them. "I saw you flare up just then and felt the force of it" is better than "I'll bet you were a terror when you were drinking!" The first is directly applicable to the patient, while the second is only a shrewd guess to which the patient can make a Baron Munchausen type of reply, knowing full well that the other was not present and therefore could not be an authority on his drinking behavior.*

Figure XV

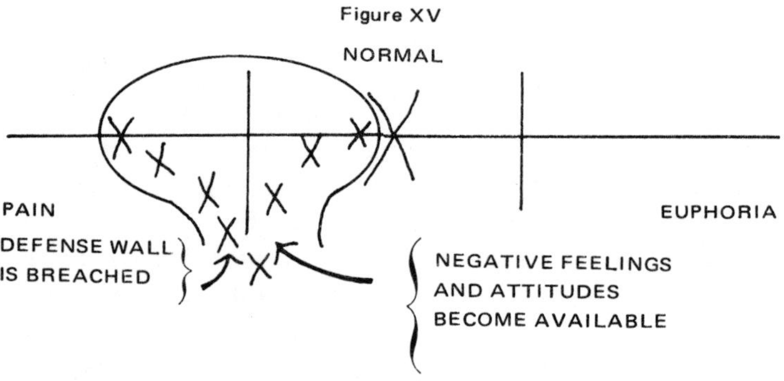

Group members are urged constantly to speak *to the available data* and to describe them carefully. "When you just said that you were not angry or upset I had a hard time believing it was true, because your face was flushed and your eyes were flashing." It is from such presentations that the patient at last comes in touch with his anger, and later on admits its presence, and still later gains the insight to know that when angry he was really *hurt,* and that the anger itself was a response to the hurt. After that, with this kind of approach, he learns more appropriate ways to deal with his "hurt feelings" than to be angry.†

*"Shrewd guessing" is also avoided because it inevitably leads to the "Let's play amateur psychologist" game and such wise statements by patients as "I think you must have had a terrible childhood!" etc., etc. Psychotherapy, when needed, is appropriate for another time, in another place, conducted by persons of qualified expertise.

†Openly and appropriately revealing that he is "hurt" comes almost always late in the intensive treatment. One who can do that is usually nearing his graduation to the outpatient rehabilitation program.

To summarize, then, the mental mismanagement and the severe emotional disorder are dealt with simultaneously. As the defenses that produce the first are recognized and accepted, they tend to break down sufficiently to allow the negative feelings to be recognized as well. This recognition makes it possible for the patient to have a new insight into his emotional condition.

8.

Characterological Conflict

"Hell, I'm a civil war!"

The patient has now improved to a point where he can be helped much more effectively. He is urged to examine his negative attitudes, to list them as they appear, and actively to search them out. Because of the intensive nature of the treatment, once this process begins it moves rather rapidly. In due time he sees his negative attitudes in profile. "I can *see* now that my emotional problems are resentment, self-pity, pride, hypersensitivity, perfectionism, loneliness, and all the rest." When he makes this admission, he is not only capable of recognizing his problems, he can actually name them. (See Appendix I.)

At this point he is asked to prepare an oral presentation of this negative profile for a session with the chaplain or one of the corps of trained clergymen who listen to the Fifth Step.* He is not only at that time to present a list of attitudes and postures which block any effective progress toward recovery, but is to support their naming with convincing evidence. For example: "I know I've become a very resentful and hostile person because I have actually been violent at home on these particular occasions." And then he must describe the incidents.

The dynamics of this experience in this vital area of treatment is a key to his recovery. He is coming to grips with the conflict within himself—his basic characterological conflicts. Very simply, this is the conflict between his values and his behavior. Whether the patient realizes it or not, he possesses deeply learned values which are central

*Of the "Twelve Steps" cited by Alcoholics Anonymous as essential to recovery, and accepted by its members. In this one, members a vow: (We have) admitted to God, to ourselves, and to another human being the exact nature of our wrongs. See pp. 90 for further reference to AA and Alanon.

to his personhood. They are his; he is committed to them. However, at this point in the disease, if he recognizes them consciously he will declare that he once had convictions but has lost them. Actually, his progressively bizarre behavior produced by the course of the illness has increasingly conflicted with these values.

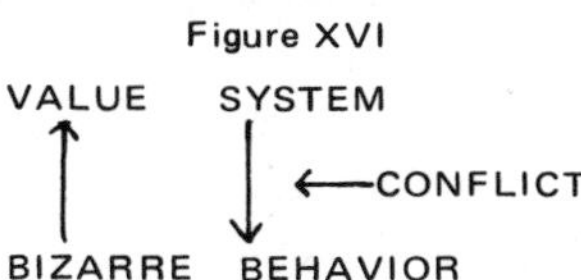

Joe's conference with the chaplain illustrates the dynamics of this phase of the treatment.

Joe came into the chaplain's office. "Well, here I am, Dave," he said, "but I'm not looking forward to this afternoon's work. I've got a real going over here. And what I've been forced to see about myself I don't like to look at at all. And now I'm supposed to tell you all about what I've discovered. Well, I can tell you first off, I'm a selfish slob! I feel so guilty about so many things I don't know where to start."

"That's as good a place as any, Joe," the chaplain said. "Just looking at you I can tell how guilty you feel, all right. Maybe you can tell me what you feel most guilty about—"

Joe thought for a second. "I feel most guilty about the way I treated my wife," he said. And then he gave a long list of specific examples of the ways he had neglected or abused their relationship. "It hurts me all the more to realize how she has taken all the resentment and self-pity I have poured on her and still stayed with me. If the situation were reversed, I know now I would have dumped her long ago. I can't believe I've done what I have done! I used to be a good husband—" Real tears were showing in his eyes.

"I can see how you feel, Joe," the chaplain said. After a pause, he quietly asked, "What do you feel next most guilty about?"

"Well, I don't think it is the *next most,* Dave, because I feel just as guilty about the way I've treated our kids during these last few years. I'd promise to take them fishing on a Saturday, and then not show up for the whole weekend. I'd come back on Monday night and offer some lame excuse why I hadn't been home. But they knew what I'd been doing.

"You know, I used to be a good father, and I guess that's why they stuck by me. At least I think they're still with me, though it's hard to believe. I can't understand what's happened to my values! I just don't *have* any values any more!" And he described other instances ignoring or of mistreating the children, and again tears filled his eyes as he finished.

"Is there something else you feel guilty about, Joe?" asked the chaplain, after another long pause.

Again a few seconds of thought. "Well, I'll tell you that I'm ashamed to go back to work and face my boss. I've been doing a half-day's work for a full day's pay for a long time now. I can't really believe he's keeping me on. You know I used to be in the top five producers, regularly, but the last two years . . ." His voice faced away as he quietly told incident after incident of how his productivity had gone down. He continued to uncover and describe his guilt with one example after another of how he had failed to meet his obligations. An hour later, he was summing it up with the same sentiment he had expressed earlier: "I can't understand how I could have changed like this. I used to be a guy who had some really high values and ideals. They've just gone out the window! I'm not the same guy. I'm not sure any more *who* I am."*

"Wait a minute, Joe. You're seeing yourself differently from the way I see you. For more than an hour you've been giving me a long list of things about which you feel terribly guilty. The meaningful way in which you've talked about yourself tells me that you really *feel* that guilt. And yet, all through this, you've kept repeating that you *used to be* a person who had values, but that they're missing now. You say you feel like nobody because your values are gone. Your values are no more gone than mine! In fact, I can tell you what they are, and even put them pretty much in the order of their importance to you.

"Your highest values are placed on being a certain kind of husband and father. I know this because it is the area of your recent life that makes you feel most guilty. And I'd have to say that you're pretty

*This personality crisis is common. The chaplain will deal with it directly to help the patient reestablish a base from which to operate. Up until now, however, he has carefully allowed the patient to *feel the full impact* of the pain accompanying the self-description. He knows that any attempt on his part to minimize this anguish would be a serious disservice to the patient and to their common therapeutic goal.

irrevocably committed to productivity, Joe. The guilt you demonstrated when you talked about your job tells me that. I could go right down the list in the order you used. The degree of guilt indicates the importance you give to these values. If your value system is really gone, Joe—how come you feel so guilty right now about these things?* You and your values never left! You're still the same person you were before you became alcoholic—your guilt feelings prove that to me."

Before Joe went away, he was already thinking hard about what his guilt feelings meant.

Before commenting on the characterological conflicts revealed by Joe's response, we note the moral anxiety and guilt brought into conscious focus by this newfound self-awareness. While this talk with the chaplain in no way is considered a confession, nevertheless, communicating with another human being in an atmosphere of trust and at depth does serve to use guilt creatively and then reduce it. Joe ended up feeling better about himself.

Another benefit of the experience was that the verbalization and capsulization of his negative behavior became an act of accepting these truths about himself, an important goal of this treatment.

The most significant advance provided by the experience, however, was that it enabled him to come to grips more consciously with the characterological conflicts within himself. He was able to recognize, even as he felt it, that the pain of his guilt was *reality* as well as a true indication that all he had once stood for had not really left him. In truth, the pain, however difficult to bear, was the proof of his sanity. People with his history should feel guilty! He recognized that he was still strongly committed to the values at the center of his identity. He had not lost his idealism.

Further, he was able to recognize that when his behavior was contrary to his values, it brought him pain. Another patient beautifully described this conflict in describing himself. "Hell, I'm a civil

*It appears that alcoholism does not exist without the presence of guilt. A basic description of chemically dependent patients is that they are *guilt-ridden people.* After the apathy caused by the factors already described disappears under treatment, guilt surfaces. There is some real question as to whether a sociopath or psychopath can be an alcoholic, since they feel no guilt about destructive behavior. The psychopath really *doesn't* care. For this reason the seriously sick chemically dependent person who appears not to care is sometimes inadvertently diagnosed as a psychopath. While he is still drinking and behaving destructively, his defenses can be so thoroughly successful as to make him look as if he feels no guilt.

Figure XVII
CHARACTEROLOGICAL CONFLICT

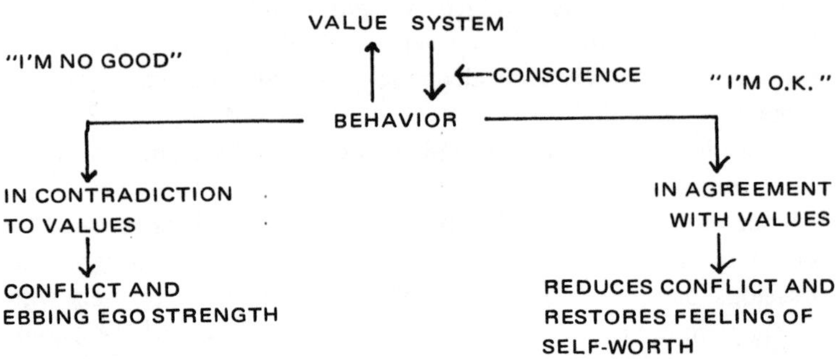

war," he commented. The concept of civil war implied a single divided entity in the battle rather than two. The struggle was between behavior and values—and both were his. He was one person in combat with himself.*

He has growing intuition that there is a way out. Behavior which is in agreement with the value system brings with it a greater sense of well-being. In fact, all sorts of intuitions began to grow. Maybe quitting the drinking would have a reward! Drinking, in the past, had promised so much, given a little, and exacted such a terrible price. In point of fact that was what he had learned to chiefly hate about himself: his drinking. Maybe if that stopped, it wouldn't be what he had thought—a bleak, dull, painful world. Maybe abstinence would actually give him a new sense of well-being. It was just an intuition at this point, but his concept of self was already starting to grow. The search for identity he had been making in the bottle started to move in a new direction. He had a glimpse of the truth that it wasn't a new self he needed, but the old self with a new way of behaving, a new life-style or something like that. He turned the corner, and a feeling long gone returned. There was hope. He was beginning to accept himself.

*As another insightful patient put it succinctly: "The alcoholic is in a clash by himself!"

9.

The Stages of Recovery

"After all, he is dry, isn't he?"

There is visible progress during the intensive inpatient period of our treatment. One can see it in the way patients behave and in the changed attitudes this reveals. We have names for the stages of progress toward recovery.

The first is *admission.* When the patient first enters the treatment unit, he is in this stage. His very presence in the treatment setting is a significant statement. By his actions he has accepted the reality that he is being treated for chemical dependency on alcohol, not gastritis or polyneuritis or even hangovers. Somewhere on a medical chart, he knows his primary diagnosis is "acute chronic alcoholism."*

It is the victim's presence in the hospital that signifies his grudging recognition of his condition. But he soon becomes capable of putting it into words. A typical self-assessment might go something like "They have me here because I got to drinking a little too much a little too often. And I guess, in some ways at least, they have a point. Maybe I was drinking too much, but I can't be alcoholic! Not really, since I still have my job, my home, and my family. If I've got this disease, I'm just in some early stage of it, because I'm still a respectable citizen, not some skid row bum."

The fact is that being in the hospital for treatment offers the distinct advantage of reinforcing the disease concept very strongly at subconscious levels. The environment itself supports this. The reinforcement

*There seems to be an anomaly in this phrase. But since all harmful chemical dependency progresses to premature death, the disease itself is viewed as an acute condition. On the other hand, since all arrested harmful chemical dependency is subject to relapse, by its very nature alcoholism is viewed as chronic—just as chronic as, say, diabetes.

is especially useful when physical complications are still minimal. The patient's response to being suddenly in a hospital is "Why, they've got me in here like I was sick or something!" His movement through the steps of *admission* is relatively easy, and therefore his comprehension of the acuteness of his mental and emotional symptoms readier and quicker. An instrument to test his ability to see and admit his condition is administered throughout this phase. (See Appendix F.)

We call the second phase *compliance.* During this period the patient's attitude changes significantly. He no longer doubts the seriousness of his condition or describes it in a weasel-worded way—he has moved to a thoroughgoing acceptance of the reality of his plight.* He is able to verbalize his problem, sometimes even vehemently. "I know I drink too much. You don't have to tell me! And you don't have to tell me that I have to quit drinking, either. I *know* that too. And I'm going to *do just that!*"

A quality of defiance is clearly evident in this sort of protestation. Although defiance is virtually always present at this stage, it is not always so readily observable. The patient may display a kind of "smiling submission" which is much more acceptable. "Oh, yes, I know I have a problem all right. That's why I'm here. Just tell me what I should do about it. I'll do anything and everything you say—within reason, of course." The defiance is subtly evident in the latter phrase. In fact, the smile may be so wide and the words so gently said that the defiance can be missed entirely. The dependence is clear, however. It is left up to the therapist to do the whole job, witness the "I'll do what you say." Even experienced counselors can be taken in by this seeming sweetness, and the inexperienced are likely to be swept into the trap. They feel the patient's dependence as the expression of a genuine need for their help. Since they cannot sense his continued defiance, they leap to the cause. "Gosh, I'd like to help him more. He's such a nice guy!" As time passes, the inexperienced counselor begins to feel guilty because he cannot "help" more, and he goes on feeling guilty. The experienced counselor may feel guilty at times, too, but sooner or later he realizes what the patient has been doing to him. As he marks the chart, "Patient still complying," the counselor's "guilt" goes away.

*Here, see T.M. Tiebout, *Surrender vs. Compliance in Therapy, with special reference to Alcoholism* (Quar. Jour. Stud. on Alc., 1953 (distributed by The National Council on Alcoholism, Inc., 2 Park Ave., New York 10016, N.Y.). All of this writer's pamphlets, by the way, are required reading in these hospitals.

Nevertheless *compliance,* as a condition, provides a real learning period in intensive treatment. Heated impromptu meetings among patients are centered around discussions of the difference between admission and compliance and compliance and acceptance (the third stage). It eventually becomes clear to the patient that compliance as a condition blocks either his genuine acceptance of the severity of his disease or his comprehension that he is being victimized by it.

We call the third phase *acceptance,* and we view achieving it as real progress. *Defiant dependence* is replaced by a kind of *wholehearted acceptance* of a personal responsibility for recovery. There is a "gut-level" insight on the part of the patient into the severity of his own symptoms, and a healthy appreciation of the fatal nature of the disease itself. "My, I was sick when I came in here—I didn't know how sick. And I certainly didn't know how serious this disease is. Why, I could have died if they hadn't insisted on my coming for treatment. Thank God they did!"

There is a buoyancy that goes with the words, almost a lilt in the tone of voice. It is an expression of gratitude, deeply felt, toward the very people who, only weeks before, had been interfering do-gooders at best, and at the worst, ogres. Damaged self-esteem has obviously been repaired, and the earlier emotional alienation from others has been replaced by increased interest and intimacy. Emotional communication comes with new openness and ease.

Now a patient is capable of saying, "You know, when you said that to me, I felt deeply hurt. What I'm trying to do now is to keep that feeling from blocking what would be a useful response to you."

The patient not only says this openly, but he can do it with a quality of sincerity and spontaneity. He demonstrates a marked increase of self-awareness, and beyond that of self-acceptance, as he says it. There is an increased *affect,* but more especially the affective behavior is in direct agreement with the words he is uttering. His body language, the expression on his face, and the tone of his voice are communicating the same message as his words, which themselves are open, accurate descriptions of him. When he says, "I'm feeling angry," he looks it and sounds it. And when he says, "I'm happy," nobody could mistake the truth of it, because of the genuineness of the smile on his face. He is believable in his presentation of himself. His interpersonal relationships are growing in depth and number. He genuinely *cares* about others. "Say, I've got to have a talk with that new guy and see how he is." He is hopeful and even at times cheerful about his future. "Thank God I got this in time!"

To the inexperienced counselor he appears ready to leave intensive care and enroll in the two-year outpatient program of rehabilitation. The experienced counselor remains wary, however; there is a quality yet missing. For one thing, the patient is still viewing his future unrealistically.

We call the fourth stage *surrender.* Here, all the welcome signs of progress from the *acceptance* phase above are present. The civil war is over, and the personality has "drawn together" again. He is open, self-accepting, warm, and willing to risk human relationships. However, the final solution of the problem is still ahead. The fact that the process is not yet complete is clearly seen in the heedless way he looks to his future.

"I've got it made now," is the attitude and feeling he is demonstrating. The chronic nature of the illness has not yet been directly or realistically faced. "Thank God, I caught this in time!" The real pressures of an abstinent life in a heavily drinking culture are being lightly waved aside as "easy" or "a cinch." He does not even consider the possibility of relapse.

When *Surrender* does come, it is signaled by an *appropriate display of caution* about the future. There is a gut-level realization that continued help during the period ahead is going to be necessary. He is cheerful with the progress to date as he says, "Well, I'm going to go out there and give it my best shot. I'm glad to know that, so far, more than 75 percent of those who have gone through this place have made it. That helps." But then he adds, "The 20-some percent who don't make it still scare me. As deep as I got into this illness, I know I'm still going to need help. I'm glad there's an outpatient program available to me, and you better believe I'm going to stick close to AA."

Now he is being realistic about the problems of his future. He is placing himself, deliberately and thoughtfully, in a position to cope more effectively with the difficulties he will surely face while he stabilizes his sobriety. He knows that, from the setting he is leaving, the chances are better than three to one that he will make it, but due caution is required nevertheless. "There is a real difference between having courage and being foolhardy." he says. "Sure I'll still need help, and I'm going to use it."

What he is now demonstrating is the beginning of another important process which needs to be further developed during his aftercare period. Even though he has "surrendered" and has realistic attitudes, there is one very basic problem he will have to work through. He will need help to deal with the rigidity in his life-style that developed during the progress of his illness. This personal rigidity is actually useful during the early phases of rehabilitation. It goes to work stopping his old self-destructive drinking pattern. He is rigid about *not* drinking.

The back of this trait of rigidity is broken by the progress he makes in the aftercare program and by his experience in AA. In the long haul, unless he learns to become even more adaptable to the unexpected environmental changes he faces, his continued sobriety will ultimately be endangered, or at the very least he will be limited in his personal relationships. The dry drunk will appear to others to have a closed mind—to be hard or brittle in certain situations. Typically, he is insistent or dogmatic in his behavior and inappropriately opinionated, holding that one way, his way, is the only way.

Even in aftercare or AA, if this quality of rigidity continues, it can reach the point where he is no longer viewed by his peers in recovery as a zealot for the program but as a "bleeding deacon" who insists loudly that "my way is the only way to make the program." They continue to endure him, more than likely, because "after all, he *is dry,* isn't he?" but they are uncomfortable with his behavior.

In any case, now he is ready to be discharged into the outpatient program of rehabilitation. This aftercare will deal in depth with rigidity and other problems that spring from the chronic nature of the disease. The initial intensive inpatient program, while it dealt directly with the acute multiphasic symptoms and reduced them as the means of arresting his disease, was also preparing him for this new period of stabilization and growth.

10.

Rehabilitation

"Just the kind of day that used to drive me to drink"

The outpatient program of therapy actually begins during the first days of intensive treatment. This happens in two ways. As soon as the patient has passed through detoxification, he starts to learn about his disease and progressively more and more about himself. In addition to comprehensive information he is given a very specific set of tools, which are immediately helpful but will also continue to be essential during outpatient rehabilitation; inpatient group therapy gets him back in touch with himself and also teaches him to trust group experiences. He now has more personal insight and can use this new skill in the outpatient group in which he expects to continue to grow. He knows the chronic nature of his illness and accepts his need to move more deeply and consistently into increasingly meaningful and open interpersonal relationships. He can take "risks." (See Appendix G.)

But there is another very basic way in which outpatient treatment begins at the inpatient level. From the beginning, careful consideration is given to the spouse. If there is a mate, that wife or husband is the other vital half of the alcoholic situation. The spouse takes part in the inpatient treatment program as an outpatient from the very start. During the first days, he or she helps provide the essential information or data that will assist in determining the severity of the illness. Later, at appropriate times, the spouse will be called upon to confront the patient's defense systems. Characteristically, when the treatment of the alcoholic has "plateaued" he may again barricade himself behind minimizing and rationalizing, and at that point the spouse can be brought in to confront him in person with "how it really was." Nevertheless, from the very beginning she (or he*) is also urged to attend every lecture possible—those in the evenings at least; to read the recommended literature carefully; and to attend the weekend orientation sessions.

She is enrolled in the outpatient "spouse" group, where she learns the goals and dynamics of group life. More especially, she learns that she herself needs help for her own emotional distress. She is confronted with her own highly developed and inordinate defense systems and negative emotional postures, and begins to recognize and accept them while the patient is in the hospital. There is the startling realization that the mate of the *wet drunk* is a *dry drunk,*—a sort of mirror image of the alcoholic. The nonalcoholic or even abstemious spouse will show almost all the symptoms of the disease except the physical deterioration caused by ethel alcohol itself.

One of her greatest problems is in the area of repression. The wife of the alcoholic has not only repressed many of her most painful memories, but more seriously, she has almost certainly repressed her negative feelings and attitudes as well. She has lost touch with herself and with the progress of her husband's disease; has increasingly exhibited inappropriate emotional and behavioral reactions to reality. Very frequently the degree of this inappropriateness is in direct ratio to repression. For example, if she has been attending Alanon (an organization for the wives of alcoholics) during the last years of her husband's drinking, she may have completely misunderstood the true goals of that very helpful organization. She may actually seem to believe that repression is the chief goal of Alanon therapy!

If a wife with this problem were asked by a counselor, "How are you feeling these days?" she would give a startling answer. She would reply, "Oh, so much better that I can't tell you! At these meetings I go to they've taught me to ignore my husband. It's his problem—not mine—if he wants to drink himself to death.† Why, if he stays out all night, I just don't pay any attention to him—I don't let it bother me *at all!*"

*It must be kept clearly in mind that the "spouse" is almost as frequently a man. Although for reasons of space we cannot deal here with both sexes in both roles, and must use the slightly more typical situation as a model, some indication of the differences in emphasis when the roles are reversed may be found in the footnote on p. 105.

†The truth is that it *is* his problem, but she misses the point and goes all the way in repressing negative feelings to harmful levels.

The key to the fact that she is fully repressing is in the words "at all" and in the way she is saying them. She sounds as though she believes it is true, while of course her husband's behavior does bother her deeply—more deeply and more harmfully now, because she is repressing the feelings of rejection and resentment down so deep that she is unconscious of their presence. What the group has been trying to point out to her is that she must change her attitude and relationship to her husband. She must stop assuming responsibility for her husband's behavior. She must realize that her own compulsive manipulations to cover up and accommodate his behavior have been, and are, quite futile. Indeed, they have only added to her own frustrations and aggravated his illness. She has to look at herself and stabilize her emotional life so that she can cope realistically with her problems. But she has misunderstood and oversimplified that message so that it reads: You have got to learn to ignore and/or forget it.

If this condition continues to develop, she reaches the point where she actually says, "I couldn't care less, whatever happens to him." Whereas of course all sane persons do care when the very structure of their established lives is being seriously threatened. If it were true that she did not care, it would be a mark of illness not of health. What she must learn is not how to be careless, but how to care and still cope. She must deal with herself and her problems, one of which—while she remains married to him—is her responsibility *to* rather than *for* her husband's sick behavior. It is when this last insight comes to her* she finally exclaims, "Why, I know now that I need help just as much as my husband!"

Once the wife admits that she too needs help, the dynamics and depth of her own personal insights run parallel to those of her husband, who is going through intensive care as an inpatient. She is also equipped, at the intellectual level, with a new body of information concerning the nature of harmful chemical dependence and how insidiously and disastrously it affects those living closely with it.† She is now ready to start work with her own emotional distress and mental mismanagement.

*Which is Step One of the Twelve.

†Every now and again this process reveals what we call a "double-header." The spouse is uncovered as being harmfully dependent herself and enters inpatient treatment. A few of those attending Alanon meetings have suddenly and unexpectedly appeared at AA meetings instead with the announcement: "I've discovered that I belong here instead of across the hall. I know now that I've got to quit drinking too."

So now, equipped with new insights, and new skills for applying them, both the chemically dependent person and the spouse enter the outpatient treatment program together. They will meet once a week for up to two years under the supervision of trained counselors.

Here the life-style of the group remains pretty much the same and needs no further description in depth. Continued growth of intrapersonal insight remains as a goal, and the question "How did that make you feel?" is often heard. Members routinely confront each other's behavior as it is occurring. Leveling with a description of one's own feelings at a given moment is relatively commonplace (a far cry from the earlier days of inpatient treatment). As in the inpatient period, new arrivals help to keep the group from becoming dynamically incestuous. Altogether there is a kind of "We know what we are doing and we know how to do it" atmosphere.

When the treatment was centered around the effort to move the patient toward reality, the basic inpatient goal was to develop deeper personal insight. This meant reducing self-delusion. The first and most essential outpatient goal becomes the development of accurate empathy as a means of achieving deeper and more meaningful relationships. This capacity is a hallmark of healthy living as well as a bulwark against relapse. To put it exactly, the goal is to help the patient learn to discern accurately what his own behavior does to the other person emotionally.

It is essential to know one's own feelings at a given moment, but in a life in relationship it is necessary to sense with equal accuracy the feelings of the other person. More particularly, it is important to recognize how one's own behavior influences someone else's emotional response. Obviously, the presence of the spouse enhances the learning opportunity. Now the common question is not "How did that make you feel?" but rather, "How did what you just said make *her* feel?"

It is obvious, of course, that without personal insight empathy is impossible. One must be in touch with one's own feelings in order to have any real appreciation or understanding of another's. The inpatient experience in group therapy was essential as preparation. But notice that it is not simply a matter of recognizing one's own and the other person's feelings. It is necessary to be able to do that *and then be able to pick the most appropriate from all possible behavior.* By behaving properly, a person can meet his own needs and the other person's as well. The goal is not a single but a triple one. It is: (1) to know oneself at a feeling level; (2) to know the feelings of others; and (3) to combine these insights for the benefit of both. Personal insight leads to the ability to be accurately empathetic;* which in turn leads to the ability to choose appropriate actions; which leads finally to deepening interpersonal relationships. Appropriate behavior is defined as that which meets some of both persons' needs; it is made possible by the simultaneous perception of those needs.

This training in empathy provides great support for the couple during the difficult days that follow discharge from the hospital. For example, let's say that Joe is two weeks home from the hospital, and as he comes in the door after work one night he has that look on his face. She has seen that expression many times in the past and has learned to recognize it as a sign that he is going to start drinking again. In the past, before his hospitalization, she has instinctively repressed the fear aroused in her by that look. (She had hidden it from herself so that she could have a more comfortable evening.) While the immediate feeling had eased through this repression, it had really generalized into a vague but nonetheless poignant dread. "I guess it won't happen tonight, but it sure is going to happen sometime soon—" And she had lived in dread, not just for an evening but for days on end. That's how it was before treatment.

Now it is different. Now, when she sees that face and feels the fear, she recognizes it as fear. From her newly gained insight comes the realization that she had better deal with the fear *now*, by leveling with it. "Joe, when you came in the door just now, you had that look on your face you always used to have just before you went on a bender. And I'm scared!"

Obviously, this is a more useful thing to do with fear than to repress it. Verbalization tends to reduce it. Or at least keeps it at a workable level. This is how it is with personal insight. It helps. But notice, at this early point in outpatient care, that neither of them can empathize with any real skill. She still does not know what that look demonstrates as to Joe's emotional state in his post-treatment condition. She is simply meeting her own needs by responding to the conditioning of the past. So far, she is not considering two crucial questions: "What does that look mean now in this new situation?" and "How does the

*Some of the so-called sensitivity groups seem to stop with the goal of personal insight as though this were in and of itself the answer. The freedom gained in this limited way sometimes leads to what is purely self-serving behavior, and meaningful relationships suffer or die.

way I am presenting myself affect his emotions?"

Their exchange might therefore continue in this fashion: What his wife has just said Joe interprets to mean that she is just as suspicious as ever. He is hurt, but spontaneous anger covers the hurt. He recognizes the anger, and remembers that he too should deal with it now by leveling. "When you get suspicious, *I* get angry, and that's what I am right now!"

She replies, "Now that outburst just makes me *more* scared of what's going to happen—"

Joe shouts, "That does it!" and stomps upstairs, still more hurt and angry.

In this setting each of them, of course, is dealing with reality in one sense. They feel what they feel and they are reporting it openly. This is a gain over the way they used to play the game of hiding their true feelings and brooding over them. The real feelings stay out in the open where they are workable, whereas before they simply festered.

The fact is that they are dealing with reality, but unfortunately only half of the reality present in their relationship. The missing half is in the other person. What if each were to show empathy and let that play its important part?

It goes differently if either one of them is empathetic, of course, but let us say that both of them are.

Joe comes into the house and his face has that look. She sees it and feels a fear of which she is aware, which she knows should be openly shared. But in the split second before she speaks, she wonders to herself, "Maybe in this new situation he is just awfully tired. I'd better check that out before I say what I feel—" and she asks, "Was it a tough day? You look a bit done in."

Joe looks at her, realizes her worry from her tone, and replies, "Yeah, it was tough all right—just the kind of day that used to drive me to drink!" Then, because he becomes aware that he has alarmed her, he quickly adds, "But you don't need to worry, hon. The one good thing about the day is that I knew I could cope with it without booze, and believe me that's a great feeling."

She in turn is empathetic enough to realize that the "great feeling" is really there as he expresses it. She is relieved and says, "Joe, you've just pushed away the fear I had when you came in the door. Thanks a lot for that—"

On his part he knows the gratitude is real and feels supported by it, and the relationship continues to grow. Instead of coming to an impasse which insight alone could not avoid, they have both used accurate empathy and have enhanced their relationship. Moreover, the personal need of each of them is effectively met.

Obviously, such empathetic skills take time to develop, and this is one of the chief reasons that a rehabilitation period of up to two years is suggested. We recommend that the patient attend Alcoholics Anonymous and Alanon meetings, either at the hospital or in the neighborhood, from the very beginning of outpatient care.* Both night and day meetings are available, and we believe that the efforts of these groups have done much to sustain our relatively high rate of recover. We will not go into the contribution of AA or Alanon in this book—the value of their programs is well proven and long established throughout the land. Their unusual and selfless cooperation can be counted on always, and *is* counted on to support our program of treatment.

AA and Alanon help sustain the parents, but frequently the older children of alcoholics also need therapy. They are encouraged to enter treatment programs on an outpatient basis. Two kinds of groups and approaches are widely available to them. Alateen groups, designed like the AA and Alanon family groups, have been organized for these young people. These meet weekly and the Twelve Suggested Steps are presented to the members. Alateen is a crucial organization in the fight against a disease that affects the whole family.

Another youth group named TK provides a program that is similar to our treatment program for adults. The affected teenagers and younger children need to recognize their defensive life-styles and free-floating negative attitudes. They also need to improve communication skills. These needs are particularly evident in young people because adolescence itself puts stress on these areas. During this period of development there is frequently a search for identity. Living with alcoholism, however, has the effect of obscuring identity and deepening the problem. The stereotyped exchange between a relatively healthy parent and child runs: "Where are you going?"

"Out."

"When will you be back?"

"Oh, sometime!"With alcoholism in the picture, there is likely to

*One very interesting development in AA is the May-Day squad. This is an AA rescue team whose members are available twenty-four hours a day to visit any outpatient who is relapsing. "Just call 'May-Day' if you need help now."

be no conversation at all. Virtually all these young people are pretty much guilt-ridden. They all ask themselves, "What did I do to get Dad to drinking like that?" Or if they are able to reject such a thought intellectually, they nevertheless feel worthless. "I tried to help, but it never worked. I really don't count much with them." They are self-pitying. "Why can't our house be like my friend's?" And they are resentful. "I can't wait till I get old enough to get out of this mess—" They are ashamed. "I can't bring my friends home to this!"

Being deprived of the loving attention of their parents has seriously debilitating effects on children. The feelings of uniqueness, separateness, or aloneness can themselves be devastating. Meeting with others of the same age who have the same problems is in and of itself a tremendous help. The length of time that children need this support varies with their condition and their progress.

Sometimes these young people are brought together with the rest of their family. This means that teenagers, their younger sisters and brothers, and their parents get intensive short-term treatment as family groups. This method has been discovered to have great benefit in reorganizing family life, which has often been severely disrupted during the ravages of the disease.

II.

Counseling Alcoholics

Dependency—Destruction—Defensiveness—Sniping

There is a practical matter of manpower which should be discussed at this point. Early in the development of our treatment, it became apparent that the outpatient groups could no longer be led by the limited professional staff. The sheer weight of numbers, with the continuous flow of graduates from St. Mary's 50 inpatient beds stretched the staff beyond its capacity. If group sizes were to be kept small enough for active and useful interchange, something had to be done. So we decided to experiment with carefully selected volunteers who would get additional training.

Thus we began the intensive training of selected outpatients who themselves volunteered for the job. Certain trainees were chosen because they already possessed useful professional skills gained from their work experience or formal education. A wide variety of skills was present in this patient population. There were medical doctors, psychologists, social workers, lawyers, and skilled administrators. But mostly, volunteers were picked because of the potential they had shown during their inpatient days. We had observed the warmth and genuineness they brought into relationships with others. Typically, they had demonstrated unusual understanding of group dynamics during their inpatient days. The intensity of the training and the required weekly attendance put their motivations to the test. A few trainees were dropped when it was realized that they had volunteered in order to meet their own needs. Others dropped out as the task became too much for them. The rest stayed. On the whole, after three years' experience, it can be claimed that the experiment was truly successful. The training is still going on, and through their years of experience these volunteer leaders have become very valuable as alcoholism counselors.

We faced another impasse as the first patients came to the end of the two-year rehabilitation period. A significant number of them simply did not want to leave their groups! This raised certain questions for the staff. Had they become so dependent on the group that they could not safely leave, or did other attachments which could be viewed as healthy create this reluctance?

We carefully reviewed each case (a procedure which has continued from that time), and on the basis of the data gathered, allowed a very few patients to remain in their groups for therapeutic reasons. The others, although it was clear that they had real and useful attachments, were encouraged to continue those attachments elsewhere. We urged them to go to AA meetings where their presence would be valuable to newcomers, or even to organize meetings in their own homes on a more informal group basis. A great many have maintained and developed friendships begun in the hospital in exactly this way. Their feelings, it turned out, were no more unhealthy than the mixed feelings of the college graduate who is both sad and glad. He is sad because he will be separated from the close friends he has made during the undergraduate years, and glad because he has passed a milestone and a new life lies ahead.

The staff must face another practical problem, created by the tensions built into the multidisciplinary design of the treatment itself. When a number of disciplines such as medicine, sociology, theology, psychiatry, and administrative skills are combined to deliver inpatient and outpatient care, the members of the team must face one reality: there are risks inherent in trying to work together, since not only will the approaches of these individuals be different—they may also conflict. Are they willing to accept this? We strongly suggest that each member of any such group be confronted with this question.

There are always tensions between physicians, nurses, psychiatrists, AA people, chemical dependency counselors, clergymen, psychologists, social workers, and all the rest. Some doctors have suspicions about AA members, and vice versa; patients may be hostile to psychiatrists; some nurses have considerable antipathy for alcoholics; and so on. These antagonisms will soon become apparent and will block effective treatment unless all members of the team have been prepared and have seriously committed themselves to the cooperative task. We know that this sort of cooperation *can* be achieved, since it has been accomplished by ourselves and other groups. However, trusting relationships do not arise automatically or even easily. Negative feelings about alcoholism have run high for generations, and whether or not professionals responsible for its treatment understand it, each discipline feels protective of its own expertise.

The attending physician perhaps must make the greatest adaptation.* He is pretty much used to giving his patients personal care. In this new setting, he must learn to trust others with much of the treatment. Most likely he has the added handicap of not having studied alcoholism in medical school. If he does adapt to this multidisciplinary treatment, he will exert a strong positive influence on the other professionals. They know that he is still the doctor, and that he is practicing in a hospital as part of a dedicated effort to make sick people well. It would be difficult to say enough good things about the medical profession's response to this new mode of treatment. Many, many physicians give spirited cooperation, and beyond this inspire the team with their eagerness to learn from others.

We have observed that all the disciplines tend to move from wary suspicion to adequate trust. Now all qualified personnel make notes on the patient's progress charts, and therefore a large body of pertinent but diversified data is commonly shared. The patient, obviously, is the one who gets the benefits.

It is important to understand that the counseling of alcoholics is a new specialty. The counselor himself is a new kind of professional. Essentially, this method of counseling falls loosely within the format of what we now call reality therapy. In this approach relatively little attention is paid to *why* the condition has come about, though in many cases that information might be useful. But lack of time prohibits it. The approach stays zeroed in on the present existence of the condition. The counselor's goal is for the patient to accept the truth that the disorder *is*—and that he *has* it. The patient has to understand all the implications of the disease and how it affects his life *now*.

The chief consideration is that he must maintain a specific regime for living if he is to survive for a normal life span. The goals, in this sense, are the same as they are for any other chronic disease. It does not really matter to the diabetic patient, for instance, why he became diabetic; his crucial need is to know what diabetes is and the regime

*In these models, the attending physician is the admitting physician, and he may be anyone on the medical staff of the hospital. The doctor is simply using the unit as he would any other service or area of his general hospital.

he must follow if he is to go on living. Diabetes is a useful illustration here, because the diabetic's regime includes what he may or may not put in his mouth. Like the alcoholic, he may decide that he is not sick after all, or that diabetes itself is not so deadly and a few pieces of cake or pecan pie won't hurt. Thus many diabetics end up in comas or dead, because their acceptance of the disease is not a surrender—i. e., a decision made at the characterological level.

The goals of the alcoholism counselor are simple and straightforward, and they deal with the realities of present and future. Some of the methods used for accomplishing these goals have been described. The one-to-one relationship needs comment. Obviously the counselor's personal qualifications to work with the dynamics of this disease go beyond his skill with mere techniques. His usefulness depends in large measure on his own personal insight and his ability accurately to divine the feelings of his patient from moment to moment. In short, he himself must be an open person, sensitive to the emotions of others. There is another requirement, too. As one trainee said, "One thing you've got to be, if you're going into this work, and that is 'weller' than the patient!"

The counselor needs both of these conditions, plus real skill in the art of communication. This becomes evident when you understand the obstacles that the typical counseling session—at least in the pretreatment and early treatment periods—routinely runs into. The patient displays distinctive characteristics which will likely appear as follows:

1. *Dependency.* He tends to enter the situation with, for what are now obvious reasons, the attitude: "You're the expert. All right, then, expert me!" An element of *defiance,* at this stage, is always present with the dependency, and both attitudes will make the counselor uncomfortable. If he does not realize that he is uncomfortable and what has made him so, he will simply react in a way that is less than useful; he is in trouble already. And the patient, who *is* the expert at manipulations, will take over the session because of his fears.

2. *Fear of destruction.* The patient's chief fear is that his presentation of himself will be destroyed. That is, he feels the counselor is out to change or correct him. (For this reason, in group therapy constant stress is laid on not trying to "fix" people). Even healthy persons in this type of setting fear strongly that exposure will result in their being taken apart or "cut up." In a highly locked-in state of the alcoholic, this attitude is greatly intensified. The patient may even use symbols

of death in describing his anxiety about the counselor. "What are you trying to do—murder me?" In any case, his fears have the effect of increasing another tendency.

3. *Defensiveness.* Since he arrives already a master of defensive warfare, the patient employs the first sessions of counseling to discover which of his defenses will likely be most useful. Then he begins to display them in force. He sees the counselor as an enemy who is out to destroy him, and his own defensive efforts very often become offensive or aggressive. This kind of approach provokes the inexperienced or unaware counselor into acting out his own needs.

The patient will play on the vulnerability of the counselor, who now sees his charge as pugnacious, unwilling to change, rebellious, uncaring for others, rigid, etc. And he responds with his own defenses to such behavior by trying to be helpful or to break through moralizing, lecturing, or otherwise trying to recapture or dominate the situation. "Don't you realize how distraught your wife has been over your actions?" or "Have you any idea what this has done to your children?" This sort of response only leads to further defensiveness, and very likely the patient begins to close in.

4. *Sniping.* That is, the patient takes sly or obvious pot shots at the counselor and the counselor's sacred cows. He has almost an instinct for the counselor's weak points or problem areas. "I suppose you and your wife get along just beautifully." or "When were *you* drunk last?" That's always a good one. If the counselor does not drink, then the obvious comment is "What would *you* know about drinking?" If he has abused alcohol, he is then open for "*You're* someone to be preaching!" In any case, at this point the counselor is likely to become defensive in turn, and not about his expertise so much as about himself.

If the process develops as described above, the relationship cannot even be started, much less developed. The patient continues to see the counselor as his enemy, and the counselor rationalizes in order to make himself feel better: "He's so sick *nobody* could help him!"

But it can happen another way, given a perceptive counselor. If he is self-aware and also accurately empathetic, he recognizes what is happening as it occurs and knows that the whole treatment effort is heading for the rocks. He sees the sets of defenses—both of them, the patient's and his own—and how they conspire to prevent him from confronting the patient with his condition. With this insight, he is free to change the course of the interview. This may happen in a variety of ways, at any stage of the process above. One very effective way is for the counselor to describe openly to the patient what is happening through a series of confrontations and levelings.

"You know, Joe, when you said, 'All right, *expert* me!' I got pretty uncomfortable because you were trying to put on me a responsibility for you which I can't accept. I know you haven't been here long enough to know how we operate our treatment, but one thing we don't do is manipulate people or force them to change." Joe then relaxes some and is less defensive.

Or he may say in reply later in the conversation, "No, Joe, we don't murder people and I'm not trying to murder you. You do tell me a lot about your real feelings when you say that, though. You feel frightened and alone, don't you?" Then Joe feels understood, and a chance for relationship opens.

Or still later, the counselor might say, "As a matter of fact, Joe, you're right! I've had quite a rough time at home. It's our oldest son. We're getting some professional help for all of us right now. When I went in there the first time to be counseled, I think I felt pretty much like you do right now—embarrassed, scared, and defiant. Right?"

He actually achieves openness, leveling, and confronting all in the same response. The patient's defenses will drop rather than rise, and counselor and patient can move together toward a healthier relationship. Common goals in the recovery pattern can then be established.

Figure XVIII

A FLOWCHART OF COLLUSION OF DEFENSES

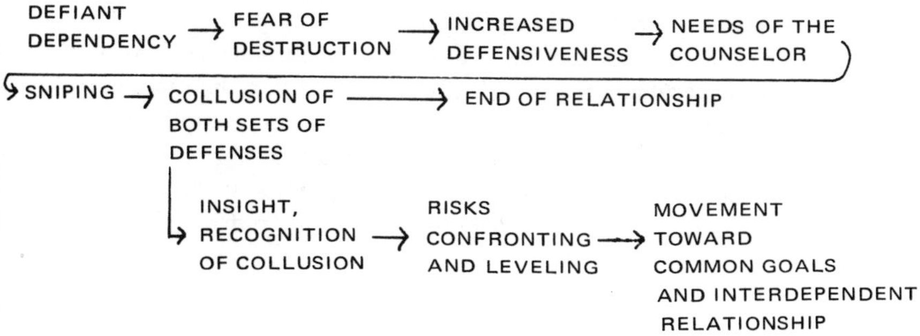

DEFIANT DEPENDENCY → FEAR OF DESTRUCTION → INCREASED DEFENSIVENESS → NEEDS OF THE COUNSELOR

→ SNIPING → COLLUSION OF BOTH SETS OF DEFENSES → END OF RELATIONSHIP

→ INSIGHT, RECOGNITION OF COLLUSION → RISKS CONFRONTING AND LEVELING → MOVEMENT TOWARD COMMON GOALS AND INTERDEPENDENT RELATIONSHIP

The great danger in one-to-one counseling with victims of this disease is the collusion of defenses. Defensiveness inevitably begets defenses in others. An experienced counselor with insight meets this situation successfully with his own ability to be open.

The method of one-to-one counseling with alcoholics has another peculiarity. Questions defeat the purpose of the therapy. Most counselors in any problem area overwork questions, but the dynamics of alcoholism are such that they really do block effective treatment. The alcoholic's inability to communicate, meaningfully or openly, constantly tempts the counselor to ask questions to get useful data. One inservice counselor trainee said, "What I have to do is to learn to ask the right questions." But on listening to the tape recording of one of his early sessions, his instructor got the instant picture of a prosecuting attorney boring in on the defendant. He wasn't questioning, he was interrogating.

Dogged and incessant questioning during one-to-one sessions can only raise defenses. Declarative sentences will help to achieve the goal of increasing the patient's openness. A remark like "Joe, I need to know more about . . ." tends to encourage a freer response. And the counselor can make effective use of leveling with an approach such as "I feel pretty handicapped, Joe, because you can't seem to tell me about the hurt you still feel inside." Or he can directly confront the patient with his own behavior, and in a concerned tone of voice tell him how he is limiting the goals of the session. "Joe," he might say, "your last comment still minimizes the seriousness of your situation, and I know you know that." The patient will usually see this as more supportive than accusing, and it will result in progress toward an interdependent relationship and more useful data flow.

In any case, the counselor's goal in these one-to-one sessions is to discover and evaluate the inpatient's progress rather than to change him. Is he moving from grudging admission toward compliance? Or is he moving from simple compliance toward a deeper acceptance? The experienced counselor will report this progress or the lack of it to the patient, in ways the latter can understand and accept.

12.
The Dynamics of Forgiveness

"He ran and fell on his neck and kissed him"

Physical complications, mental mismanagement, and emotional disorder are accompanied by a similarly progressive spiritual deterioration in the chemically dependent person. Remember, a person cannot become an alcoholic unless there is conflict between his behavior and his values. To sum up: guilt, shame, and remorse exact their inevitable and immobilizing tolls as time goes on. Feelings of self-worth consistently decline. As meaningful relationships wane or wither, the growing estrangements lead eventually to spiritual collapse. At the end intense despair and hopelessness produce suicidal moods. To the question, "Can't you see that you are drinking yourself to death?" the alcoholic answers, "So what?" or "Who cares?" And he is in fact committing slow suicide.

Of course these spiritual dynamics are not unique to this illness. All lonely, guilt-ridden, and hopeless people share the same delusion. And always there is the evasion of blame, a reaction which apparently began with Adam. As the Creation account goes, God put Adam in the Garden of Eden and gave him only one admonition: "You may freely eat of every tree of the garden; but shall not eat of the tree of the knowledge of good and evil." Adam promptly ate the fruit of this tree and immediately felt guilty and estranged, and "hid himself amongst the trees of the garden." Unfortunately for him this physical form of evasion did not work, since, as the story continues, God searched him out.

When finally confronted with his behavior, Adam was forced into more subtle forms of evasion. His response to his confrontation must be the classic rational defense of all time: "The woman Thou gavest me, she gave me to eat." Notice that it isn't just Eve who gets blamed by the first man for his own behavior. In typical fashion, he throws it all right back on the Creator Himself! "The woman Thou gavest me . . ." In effect he is saying, "Don't come to me with *your* problem. You made her that way. I didn't!" (Eve doesn't do much better with her defense: "The serpent beguiled me, and I did eat.")

Thus man's propensity to evade his responsibility for his own destructive behavior seems to have been built in and recognized since the dawn of time. Rationalizations are automatic reflexes, as it were. Alcoholism is only one of the conditions that call attention to man's evasiveness. The only difference between the effect of alcoholism and the general human condition is that with this disease there is repetitious and worsening destructive behavior. The self-deceit becomes pathological in its proportions, as it does with any other chemical dependency or addiction.

Ultimately the crux of the problem for the alcoholic and other guilt-ridden people is characterological conflict, and this basic cause is at the root of most symptoms of the disease. Both the development of the conflict and its final resolution through forgiveness are illustrated in the familiar story of the Prodigal Son. In an age when ready acquaintance with our biblical heritage is less to be counted on than formerly, we venture to set down in full this parable which contains so many insights lately rediscovered in the modern world of psychiatry and elsewhere; for they are pertinent here.

"And he said, A certain man had two sons: and the younger of them said to his father, Father, give me the portion of thy substance that falleth to me. And he divided unto them his living. And not many days after the younger son gathered all together, and took his journey into a far country; and there he wasted his substance with riotous living. And when he had spent all, there arose a mighty famine in that country; and he began to be in want. And he went and joined himself to one of the citizens of that country; and he sent him into his fields to feed swine. And he would fain have been filled with the husks that the swine did eat; and no man gave unto him. But when he came to himself he said, How many hired servants of my father's have bread enough and to spare, and I perish here with hunger! I will arise and go to my father, and will say unto him, Father, I have sinned against heaven and in thy sight: I am no more worthy to be called thy son: make me as one of thy hired servants. And he arose, and came to his father. But while he was yet afar off, his father saw him, and was moved with compassion, and ran, and fell on his neck and kissed him. And the son said unto him, Father, I have sinned against heaven, and in thy sight: I am no more worthy to be called thy son. But the father said to his servants, Bring forth quickly the best robe, and put it on him; and put a ring on his hand, and shoes on his feet; and bring the fatted calf, and kill it, and let us eat, and make merry: for this my son was dead, and is alive again; he was lost, and is found. And they began to be merry. Now his elder son was in the field: and as he came and drew nigh to the house, he heard music and dancing. And he called to him one of the servants, and inquired what these things might be. And he said unto him. Thy brother has come; and thy father hath killed the fatted calf, because he hath received him safe and sound. But he was angry, and would not go in: and his father came out, and intreated him. But he answered and said to his father, Lo, these many years do I serve thee, and I never transgressed a commandment of thine: and yet thou never gavest me a kid, that I might make merry with my friends: but when this thy son came, which hath devoured thy living with harlots, thou killedst for him the fatted calf. And he said unto him, Son, thou art ever with me, and all that is mine is thine. But it was meet to make merry and be glad: for this thy brother was dead, and is alive again; and was lost, and is found.

Virtually all the basic spiritual dynamics of alcoholism are present in the events and relationships of this story, which we will explore at some length, as presenting in a small space and almost tangibly insights that bear closely on our subjects.

A younger son asks his father prematurely for his half of the inheritance he shares with an older brother. Having received his share, he does the very worst: "He went to a far-off country" and there "wasted his substance in riotous living." It is worth noting the language here. Although this is descriptive of humanity generally, it is particularly applicable to the alcoholic. The young man wasted his substance on nothing so dull or prosaic as *evil* living, but rather on *riotous* living.

So it is with those stricken by this disease. Alcohol is first used to add zest to life. It is in no sense considered an experiment with what is evil, but rather with what is essentially *good.* The lessons learned with the first experiences are all pleasant. The goal is to enhance life —to give it more zing.

If this old story were to be told in a modern setting, one might think of the younger son going to Las Vegas, where the streets are all lighted up with beckoning neon signs. He slips into one pleasure palace after another—as one begins to pale, he moves on to the next. Then on to the dawn floor show. On down what seems like a never-ending street he goes, pursuing his rainbows to the end of the line. Finally his resources are thoroughly wasted (another word so descriptive of alcoholism).

It is in the pit of self-degradation that the turning point comes for the young man in the parable. The physical description of his environment could not be more devastating. He has been sent to feed swine. The utter shame of this condition is fully appreciated only when one remembers that he was forbidden by Mosaic law to eat the flesh of these animals or even touch it, as unclean.

In the same fashion, the chemically dependent person chases the rainbows of euphoria, seemingly heedless of the rising costs to himself and others. He is eternally hopeful that "the next time will be different." In the end, if it is allowed to progress that far, all resources are spent: health, wealth, feelings of self-worth, and all dear relationships. All he once had is laid waste; all he once was is gone. There is nothing left now but to crawl away and die. In its own way, his future role as he understands it is only to be a hired servant: for the rest of his days he will be at the beck and call of those he has hurt by his past behavior. He is to repay and repay his unrepayable debt.

What thoughts the Prodigal Son had on his long trip home we are only allowed to surmise. Undoubtedly they were excruciating, for he had no notion that he could be returning to anything he had once had or been. There was only a judgment to be faced, and some kind of repayment, however inadequate. His overwhelming need to pay a penalty is clear.

Imagine, then, his emotions during the next scene. His father saw him "when he was yet a great way off, and had compassion, and ran and fell on his neck and kissed him!" One might pass over this meeting with some shallow comment such as, "Forgiveness is wonderful! Wasn't it fine of the father to behave like that after all his son had wasted?" This is to miss the point entirely. The response of the son to his father's actions, is without question one of great shock and dismay. He says as much when he pulls back from the embrace and replies, "I am no more worthy to be called thy son!"

Far from bringing him relief, his father's greeting is a most searingly painful experience. The overwhelming shame, the remorse of his soul-searching, and the torture of the self-judgment that followed, put together, could not touch the pain of the moment when his father's arms went around his neck. This reception, one sees, is as impossible to accept as it was to imagine or foresee. He has come home immersed in his feeling of degradation. His need to be punished is not being met;

if his father would not do it for him, he would punish himself!

It is in this mood, laden with guilt, that many alcoholics plunge themselves into new and more furious drinking bouts. And here is the writhing, tormented spirit of the Prodigal.

If only his father had come out with a whip in his hand. If only his father had beaten the living daylights out of him! At the very least, if only he had made him a hired servant—that at least would have been understandable. But more than that, and here is that basic problem, it would have allowed the son to evade what he unconsciously wants desperately to evade: his final act of accepting himself as he is.

He is coming to his father specifically to disclaim what he is—a son. He is bent on being someone other than himself—a hired servant. Even if he were beaten, he could hang onto this aim. His false pride would be served if he could lift his head and claim that he had "taken his just deserts like a man," on the one hand or on the other, if he could endure whatever lengthy misery servanthood would entail. Either way he could evade what the arms around his neck demand of him: that he accept himself *as himself.*

Another insight into this spiritual dilemma is that acceptance of the father's forgiveness demands that he forgive himself. Leaving the arms around his neck, and reentering the lovingly offered relationship with his father makes it necessary that he be the person he truly is. And what is more fearful, he must go back to the way of life that sonship requires of him. He is not in a condition to do this. Even the possibility of such assumed responsibility brings shock and dismay. In effect, the alcoholic is crying out, "Don't ask me to do that! I can't accept your forgiveness because that would require that I forgive myself! Forgiving myself is impossible! And living responsibly as who I am is too much to expect!"

The intensity of the alcoholic's struggle to pass through this part of his spiritual and emotional recovery is difficult to describe, and we do not mean to exaggerate. But the importance of his doing it is almost beyond comprehension. Dynamically, this is accomplished by his movement from what was earlier defined as *acceptance* into gut-level *surrender.* It is the ultimate resolution of his characterological conflict. The central question, "Who am I?" is answered. The guilt-ridden and shame-filled admission, "I am who I am, God help me!" moves, moreover, to the more peaceful and hopeful "God help me to *be* who I am!" Of course, this may and often does, come in other words and phrases. As he surrenders, he sees that it is possible for him to risk being himself, and he moves consciously toward deepening his meaningful relationship with others because this will help him recover himself.

There, on that road, this final battle within the Prodigal is fought and apparently won. His receiving the ring on his hand, the robe, and the shoes are all symbols of the fact that his civil war is over. He is willing to be changed and to accept the responsibilities inherent in being himself, for he enters the house itself and not the servants' quarters. Without question, doubts and fears are still present. "Can I do it?" must still be answered; and the embarrassment of making amends to those who have been hurt, he intuitively knows, will be difficult and painful. Nonetheless, that he does surrender to being himself is made clear by the father when he says, "Kill the fatted calf. For this my son was dead and is alive again; he was lost and is found."

It would be a simple and happy ending if this were all there was to the story. However, other spiritual dynamics present in the disease are evident in the parable as it continues. "Now his elder son was in the fields, and as he came and drew nigh to the house, he heard music and dancing." When he inquires of a servant what is happening and learns that his brother has come, "and thy father hath killed the fatted calf because he hath received him safe and sound," his reaction is immediate, typical, violent, and understandable. In short, he is furious! "And he would not go in."

His reaction is violent and understandable because he is, in truth, the good guy in the story. The very fact that he is in the field when all this is happening is clear indication that he has conscientiously stayed with the tasks of the farm throughout. Moreover, labor has perhaps doubled with his brother's defection. He is the loyal one, the thrifty and hard-working one through all the back-breaking years.

"Lo, these many years do I serve thee, neither transgressed I at any time thy commandment." This elder brother is the very paragon of virtue, and one must agree that his indignation is both natural and justifiable. He is the fellow who kept things going, got up with the alarm, came back from the field dead tired, went to bed at a decent hour, and got up and did the same thing all over again the next day. He has a right to be indignant.

But notice the quality and depth of his indignation, and you will recognize the severity of his emotional and spiritual problem. In effect he shouts, "Never *once* did I stray from the straight and narrow path, and I didn't get so much as a baby goat, much less a fatted calf, for my trouble! But this so-and-so, after all he's done, comes back and gets a celebration!" The elder brother is more than just furious: he is filled with resentment, self-pity, and self-righteousness—loaded with pride, jealousy and no doubt envy. One can hear him thinking, "If there's no reward for being good, then why was I? If I'd known fifteen years ago what I know now, I'd have been out there with him! He's having his cake and eating it too."

His father entreats him: "It was meet that we should make merry and be glad, for this thy brother was dead and is alive again!" But to no avail, for forgiveness is not only difficult, in these circumstances, it is unthinkable. The elder brother has been hurt too often, too long, and too deeply.

Obviously, this describes many emotions of the family or other meaningful people around the alcoholic. Their spiritual and emotional distress is precisely the same, the only difference being the degree. The spouse daily bears the burden of the alcoholic's progressive defection from his responsibilities. She has to take over both roles: mother and father. Eventually, she becomes the planner, even in many cases the provider. She does it conscientiously and consistently. She bears the responsibility for decision-making. She keeps things together somehow—And as the alcoholic projects his self-loathing upon her, she is frequently verbally abused and insulted for her very selflessness.

She does her best to shield him and their problems from the rest of the community. She covers up for him in every possible way. She lies for him to employers and relatives and neighbors, all at great cost to her self-esteem. She comes to believe finally that, while others may live and enjoy life in normal ways, she must live for others, and that somewhere—somehow—there must be adequate reward for such sacrifice.*

And then, after all this, he goes to the hospital and she is told that he is coming back well again, ready to start life over *and capable of*

*It has been noted that nearly half of these spouses are husbands. The dynamics of their problem are basically the same. They feel guilty, shamed and fearful as they return home from work and repeatedly find their wives intoxicated. They tend to cover for these wives by hiding the problem from parents and family. A difference, however, does seem to occur in that the wives are not forced into the public eye by jobs, and their drinking, being in the home, stays hidden *longer.* They become sicker, it seems, before intervention is at last attempted by husbands who are desperate. The withdrawal from social and family activities becomes more severe with many of these wives who simply "draw the shades and cease to answer the telephone."

doing it! Quite apart from all her other concerns—not the least of which are her basic personal inadequacy and her fears that this may be just another false hope—she is now told she is to overlook the past and forget it. It's too much! Forgive, after all the suffering he's caused —impossible!

Forgiveness is costly, and these costs are too often minimized, or forgiveness itself is confused with repression. "I'll forgive you, but I can never forget it," or "I'll try to forget it, but I'll never be able to forgive you," are statements which ignore the basic elements required in forgiveness. What are the problems of each of these two "brothers" that must be solved if forgiveness is to be real?

Both must pay a personal cost if there is to be a restored relationship. The "younger brother" must first identify *specifically* the destructive behavior that strained or ruptured relationships. He must work out a list of his offenses: he did this particular thing, and this, and this, and as a result his brother suffered. He must not only recognize and admit his fault in these matters, but also accept the fact that it is his responsibility to start the action that will mend the break. In the context of the parable, he cannot stay in the house and allow his father to do the entreating of the older brother. He must go out and do it himself, no matter what it costs him in embarrassment or shame. He must admit his blame to his brother personally and offer whatever amends are appropriate. The *personal cost* must be paid.

While these requirements apply to all people whose behavior destroys relationships, they are likely to be a life-and-death matter for the alcoholic. Others may survive disclaiming actual and legitimate blame for their actions, but the alcoholic cannot. He cannot evade responsibility, for his own sake as well as for the sake of others, since his future quite literally depends on restoring and maintaining adequate feelings of self-worth. Those feelings will be present in direct proportion to the degree of personal responsibility with which he conducts himself as he lives with others.* Hopefully, useful relationships which have been broken will be restored by such responsible behavior, but even though certain ones may never be recovered, his sincere efforts to make adequate amends will serve to keep his own internal condition at a healthy level.

One can see the younger son running out of the door when he hears

*Steps Eight and Nine in AA clearly have taken these dynamics into account.

of his brother's reactions. And as the brother strides angrily away from the house, hurrying after him, explaining as he goes that he understands completely why he feels as he does. The younger brother assumes responsibility for his own actions, and initiates the reconciliation.

The costs of forgiveness, in at least one sense, are greater and more difficult for the elder brother to pay. In order to be a forgiving person, what the injured person must do goes far deeper than merely saying, "I forgive you." If the process is to be real he has to identify himself with the behavior of the one who has done the injury just as though it could have been his own. "There, but for the grace of God, go I!" is a truth that he must be able to accept at a meaningful level. (See Appendix I.)

Moreover, if he is to be truly forgiving he will be forced to look at, recognize, and accept certain specific negative attitudes and postures within himself. And he must work out these problems if he is to regain spiritual and emotional balance in his own life. This is particularly difficult, since the injured party almost never feels any responsibility for the situation or for his own negative attitudes.

He sincerely believes the other person has created the situation and that his own attitudes are the inevitable result. The other person is therefore responsible for them. Given this belief, he even has great difficulty in accurately identifying his own feelings. Deep resentment he sees, for example, as righteous indignation (hence justifiable). The same is true of self-pity or envy or any other of a long list of negative attitudes that keep him miserable.

And the problem is compounded because, whatever the elder brother feels, he believes himself to be thoroughly justified in feeling it. It is someone else's problem to change his feelings. He does not realize that his own emotional and spiritual conflicts are self-destructive in effect. Notice who is in the house and who is out, at the end of the story. While it is not specifically stated, the elder brother may be presumed to be stalking out toward the horizon, in justifiable indignation. He may even be turning his unrecognized self-pity and envy into hatred for a forgiving father as well as a wastrel brother. The end result is his own personal estrangement.

So it is with the extremely distressed spouse or other meaningful person. Emotionally and spiritually she is, more often than not, locked into an inability to recognize the nature of her own distress. She resists help, because "It is his problem, not mine. When he straightens up, I'll be all right!" Even if she does recognize certain negative attitudes and positions of her own, for the most part she is able quite successfully to justify them.

"If you had to live with what I've had to live with these last years, you'd be indignant and angry too," she says. She is feeling really deep resentment strongly tinged with self-pity, but does not recognize these emotions. "I've been giving and giving all these years—I don't see why I should have to keep on doing it" (again registering self-pity and resentment). The wife is apt to deny strongly that she has any need to identify with destructive behavior, although of course she shares a capability for it along with the rest of the human race. But to her the comparison is invidious and unfair. "I wouldn't be caught dead doing what he's done!" The price of forgiving comes high, because it forces the forgiver, also, to *accept* his or her own failings and destructive attitudes as needing similar forgiveness.

The cost of forgiveness is great in still another area. In order to be real, forgiveness carries with it the need for a restored trust in the reestablished relationship. But how can one trust what has a history of being impossible to trust? The many broken promises of the past come flooding back into memory and the spouse shakes her head sadly as she says, "I'd like to trust you this time—I really would, but I can't. All those times when I had such high hopes, only to have them knocked over—the memories get in my way. How can I say I forgive you when I still can't trust you?"

The apparent problem here really has another and deeper spiritual core. At the obvious level, the recovering alcoholic sees simply that his wife is untrusting or distrustful of him. This is thoroughly frustrating, because he must agree with her logic: his past behavior can in no way inspire trust. He sees progress at a standstill, and he faces a postponement of any really meaningful relationship with her until the passage of time awakens trust in her once again, if that is possible. In any event, it is not her problem, it is his. It is all up to him to prove something to her.

She sees it the same way. There is nothing she can or should do to speed up the process or to cause it to occur. What she does not realize is that there is a side to it which does involve her and her alone. If she does not recognize her own problem, the trusting relationship may not only be delayed, but may be put off forever.

The deeper and unrecognized truth may well be that she not only does not trust him, but in addition does not trust herself to be hurt once again.* The cost of trusting another whose behavior has a history of being untrustworthy is to take the risk of being hurt—that is, to *trust oneself* in deliberate exposure to the possibility of being hurt again. This is the spiritual problem the spouse must face and work through.

If the costs of forgiveness are great, so are the rewards. Forgiveness can mean not only restored and more meaningful relationships, but also strengthened and more matured individual lives.

For the alcoholic, the effect of directly admitting his culpability is just as directly beneficial to him as it is to the spouse. "Oh sure, I must have been out of my mind when I did those things, and I know now that I was so deluded that I *was* out of my right mind. Nevertheless, I did them! I'm responsible for the hurt they caused." Thus feeling and acknowledging remorse is helpful to him as it is to his wife and everybody else in the relationship.

The same may be said of his taking restorative action. As he is able to make things up to other people and repay them, he restores himself. His self-image, so badly damaged during the course of the illness, is being repaired; his ego strength is being enhanced. He feels better about himself—which is to say, he is more self-accepting. While he is accepting forgiveness from another, he is being placed in a position where he can more easily and thoroughly forgive himself. His character conflicts can more easily be reduced. In turn, he is therefore better able to accept (or forgive) someone else.

All the meaningful people who have suffered with the alcoholic gain significant benefits from this whole process. Identifying with the other person's behavior, as well as with that person, makes a tremendous closeness possible. The wife may truthfully say, "We haven't been this close before in our whole marriage." She too feels better about herself; she too is more self-accepting. In forgiving another, she has forgiven herself as well.

Finally, all this deep acceptance of each other tends to provide a spiritual climate in which individuals can become increasingly self-aware and empathetic. The family learns to recognize such continuing attitudes as resentfulness, pride, and self-pity as destructive. As the members are more able to communicate with each other they can deal

*The experienced counselor will probe for this condition until it is recognized and brought out into a workable position. "You learned to be trusting all those other times, and you survived even the bitterest disappointment. What's one more time?"

directly with these feelings and can often reduce them.

At the same time the family will be seeking out and nurturing such attitudes as care, love, concern for others, faith, compassion, and gratitude. In families where recovery is successful, a truly new life may begin. Parents and children will find a new affection in their understanding and trust of each other, a new depth in their open communication with each other. This is the true goal of the whole process of treatment.

One survivor felt he had been blessed by this whole new life. "Thank God, I'm an alcoholic!" he said. "I just might have missed knowing and appreciating life as it is now."

APPENDIXES

Appendix A

PATIENTS' HANDBOOK

Welcome

You are a patient in this two-year treatment program because you are sick with a chronic addiction—that is, a harmful dependency on a chemical substance which interferes with your daily life.

Because your condition is chronic, you cannot be cured. But you can be treated successfully.

Our treatment objective is two-fold: to arrest your disease and to recover your person.

While you are an inpatient, you will be safely withdrawn from all chemicals, treated for the immediate symptoms of your illness, and you will initiate your personal recovery.

Upon discharge from the hospital, you will continue treatment as an outpatient for a period of two years. This extended care is necessary both to assure full recovery of your person and to minimize the danger of relapse.

Rehabilitation—that is, organizing a new way of life with new patterns of living and thinking—is your primary purpose in treatment. Upon satisfactory completion of inpatient treatment, you will be able to lead a normal life, free from chemicals, provided you embrace and continue the therapy offered to you as an outpatient.

Your unreserved cooperation is essential to your recovery. Mere compliance, going through the motions without internal acceptance and personal motivation, will leave you sick.

You will find the atmosphere friendly and our personnel understanding of your condition and problems. You will gain much support from fellow patients and will be able to contribute much toward their recovery, both during and after your residence here.

Treatment Program

Patients admitted to this Center participate in a two-year therapy program. The staff will in each individual case determine the date on which the patient enters effectively into treatment and the date on which the patient is ready to be transferred to the outpatient phase of treatment.

A. Phases of Treatment

Phase One. *Observation and Detoxication*

Upon admission to The Chemical Dependency Treatment and Rehabilitation Center you will be placed under the close observation of the medical and nursing staffs for as long as required to:

1. Insure your safe and complete withdrawal from alcohol and/or other mood-changing chemicals.
2. Examine your general state of health.
3. Determine the extent to which other hospital services may be necessary during your treatment period.

Phase Two. *Inpatient Treatment*

After withdrawal, you will enter a period of inpatient therapy designed to help you:

1. Identify your illness.
2. Accept your condition as a chronically diseased person.
3. Formulate your personal rehabilitation program.
4. Continue medical treatment as needed under the care of your private physician.
5. Become familiar with the Twelve-Step Program of Alcoholics Anonymous, which in practice has been proven effective.

Phase Three. *Outpatient Treatment*

Because harmful chemical dependence is a chronic condition, each patient is to remain in weekly contact with the nonmedical program of treatment for a period of time up to two years after inpatient discharge. Continuing group experiences are designed to meet special problem areas in the initial stages of recovery. You will be expected to return to the Chemical Dependency Treatment and Rehabilitation Center for:

1. A weekly therapy session.
2. Consultation and counseling with staff members as required for your continued successful recovery and rehabilitation.

For a continuing program of recovery, outpatients, spouses, and families are expected to attend:

1. Weekly Alcoholics Anonymous meetings in your community.
2. Weekly Alanon meetings for the spouse.
3. Weekly Alateen meetings for the teenagers.

B. Elements of Nonmedical Inpatient Treatment

I. *Education*

Through 54 lectures, selected films, and prescribed readings, you receive current and accurate information concerning:

1. The nature and dynamics of your progressive and chronic disease.
2. The physical, social, and personality deteriorations which accompany it.
3. The basic understanding of a method for achieving and maintaining a comfortable way of life free from further dependence upon mood-changing chemicals.

II. *Group Therapy*

Repeated experiences in groups of people who suffer from the same affliction provide you with encounters designed to confront and break down defense mechanisms and negative attitudinal postures which always accompany chemical addiction.

Group therapy enables you to recognize and accept:

1. Who you are.
2. Which specific attitudes and behavior patterns must be modified in order to live comfortably without dependence on harmful chemicals.

III. *Individual and Family Counseling*

Particular life problems vary from patient to patient, and other members of your family are inevitably involved in the disruptions caused by your illness. Therefore both individual and family counseling are viewed as essential to successful rehabilitation.

Multidisciplinary Treatment

Alcoholism and other chemical dependencies are chronic diseases affecting the total personality and all the interpersonal relations of its victims. Chemically dependent persons typically suffer progressive deterioration of physical, emotional, mental, and spiritual health. Their addiction to mood-changing chemicals produces this havoc.

A life free from all chemicals is difficult to achieve. For the addict, it is a terrifying prospect. Lacking inner security, he grows overly dependent upon external things and people, demanding of them support they cannot provide. As these fail him, he turns to chemicals increasingly until they not only fail to sustain him, but enslave him, dominating his entire life. Unless and until he achieves personal integrity and attains inner security, he is powerless to live free from chemicals.

No one specific treatment has been discovered which is capable of producing these requisites for recovery. Therefore, to successfully arrest alcoholism a total, multidisciplinary treatment is necessary; involving medical, behavioral, and social science, and philosophical and theological wisdom.

Responsibilities of Patients on Unit

1. Each patient is responsible for attendance at all lectures, films, group therapy sessions, and Alcoholics Anonymous meetings.
2. Each patient is responsible for attendance at all meals.
3. Each patient is responsible for making his bed and arranging his room in an orderly manner every morning. This can be done between breakfast and the morning lecture.
4. Each patient, when leaving the unit, is responsible for signing in and out in the book provided on the nursing station. Leaving the unit or hospital premises, except for grave reasons, is contrary to treatment procedures because it interferes seriously with the recovery of patients. This includes visiting patients and/or receiving visitors in other parts of the hospital.
5. Each patient is expected to assume responsibility for daily tasks as assigned.
6. A pay phone is available for urgent calls. Since outside contacts delay the progress of treatment, each patient is responsible for keeping these to a minimum.
7. A special time for study and reflection is provided daily from 4:00 P.M. to 5:30 P.M. This time may be used profitably to study assigned reading, prepare your First Step material, take your Fourth Step Inventory, prepare for your Fifth, or meditate. Respect for the privacy of others during these hours is a personal responsibility of each patient.
8. Roommates and fellow patients are expected to be helpful in orientating new patients to the unit and helping them to get acquainted.
9. Concerned persons and/or spouses may visit and attend lectures with patients each evening after *7:00 P.M.*

   Relatives and friends are welcome to visit patients every Sunday from *2:00 to 4:00 P.M.* All other visiting of patients will be by special arrangement with the treatment staff.
10. Each patient is responsible for being real, leveling with his own feelings, and confronting fellow patients' irresponsible behaviors—at all times.
11. Each patient is responsible for keeping himself in good physical condition. Sports equipment is available.
12. Reading list—follows.

Reading List

1. *Arresting Alcoholism,* Christopher D. Smithers Foundation, 41 East 57th St., New York, N.Y. 10022

2. *Experimentation* (the fallacy of "controlled" drinking where alcoholism exists), Christopher D. Smithers Foundation, 41 East 57th St., New York, N.Y. 10022

3. *Alcoholics Anonymous* (the basic text for Alcoholics Anonymous, 2nd edition), Alcoholics Anonymous World Services (and) AA Grapevine, Box 459, Grand Central Station, New York, N.Y. 10017

4. *Twelve Steps and Twelve Traditions,* Alcoholics Anonymous World Services (and) AA Grapevine, Box 459, Grand Central Station, New York, N.Y. 10017

5. Harry M. Tiebout, M.D., *The Ego Factors in Surrender in Alcoholism,* National Council on Alcoholism, 2 Park Ave., New York, N.Y. 10016

6. Harry M. Tiebout, M.D., *Surrender Versus Compliance in Therapy,* National Council on Alcoholism, 2 Park Ave., New York, N.Y. 10016.

7. Harry M. Tiebout, M.D., *Conversion as a Psychological Phenomenon,* National Council on Alcoholism, 2 Park Ave., New York, N.Y. 10016.

8. *Guide to Fourth Step Inventory* and *Guide to Fourth Step Inventory for the Spouse,* Hazelden, Center City, Minn. 55012.

9. John Powell, S.J., *Why Am I Afraid to Tell You Who I Am?,* Peacock Books, Argus Communications, 3505 N. Ashland Ave., Chicago, Ill. 60657.

10. John Powell, S.J., *Why Am I Afraid to Love?,* Argus Communications, 3505 N. Ashland Ave., Chicago, Ill. 60657.

11. Vincent P. Collins, *Me, Myself and You,* Abbey Press, St. Munrad, Ind. 47577.

Appendix B

GROUP THERAPY HANDBOOK

The purpose of this paper is to discuss the assumptions and techniques we are using in conducting group therapy. To begin with, let's look at some of the similarities within our group. In addition to our alcoholism we all have two things in common. First, before we came to the point of seeking outside help, we each tried our own *do it yourself* program in an effort to change ourselves. The second similarity is that we all failed. A basic assumption of group therapy is that a major reason for this failure is that our most determined efforts can't change what we can't see, and that there is a great deal that we are not seeing clearly.

For this reason our *goal* in group therapy is:

To discover ourselves and others as feeling persons, and

To identify *the defenses that prevent this discovery.*

While change is the ultimate goal, our immediate purpose is to see more accurately what needs change. This requires seeing ourselves—*discovering ourself*—and at a feeling level.

In examining our purpose one of the things that stands out is our emphasis on feelings. We stress feelings for several reasons. First of all, our behavior in the past has been so opposed to our value system that considerable feelings of remorse and self-loathing have been built up. It appears that we have accumulated a pool of negative feelings and walled them off with a variety of masks or *defenses that prevent this discovery.* This began with mild disapproval of ourself, then growing remorse, and finally a deep self-loathing. Statements such as: "I'm no damn good!" or "The world would be better off without me," reflect these negative feelings and attitudes. It is important to be in touch with these in order to take the First Step of the Alcoholics Anonymous Program where: "We admitted that we were powerless over alcohol—that our lives had becomes unmanageable."

Being in touch with the hostile feelings we have toward ourselves and the sense of helplessness and hopelessness that accompany them, make the First Step a moving a description instead of simply an abstract theory. We *feel* the *powerlessness* and the *unmanageability.* One of the important functions of the group is to help us *identify the defenses that prevent this discovery.* We will say more about this wall of defense later on.

Another reason for stressing feelings is that many of the character defects that have disabled us for years are reflected in our feeling states or attitudes. As a result of the conflict between our value system and our repeated chemically-induced behaviors, we have formed rigid negative feeling states called attitudes toward ourselves and others. Most of us have become one or more of the following persons: Hostile, Resentful, Angry, Self-pitying, Fearful, Defiant, Phony, Arrogant, Superior. While these are represented as feelings, some have become so thoroughly a part of us as to be attitudinal in nature. They substantially color the way we see life and react to it. No longer are we persons who simply at times feel resentment; we are resentful persons. We may discover that we are not simply persons who feel self-pity; but we have become self-pitying persons. What was once a feeling has now hardened into an attitudinal posture —a character defect. If we are to change we must first become ourselves at this feeling level.

Most of us are badly out of touch with our feelings, particularly the ones we have been describing. But as you will see, it is not just these negative feelings that are hidden and controlled. Our positive feelings of joy and love are also locked away by the defenses that seek to hide the negative feelings from view. It appears that our defenses are not selective. The man who has hidden away his anger is also crippled in any spontaneous display of affection or gratitude as well. While our main focus in group therapy is on identifying our destructive negative-feeling selves, the acceptance of these feelings frees the positive ones as well. "I never could tell anyone I really liked him before, unless I was drinking," is one example of this phenomenon.

Most of us have ignored our feelings for years in an effort to see the facts. In group therapy *feelings are facts.* "How does that make you feel?" is a question asked frequently to help us focus on these facts.

Since our feelings are new to us, let's look at the ones we use everyday: Mad, Sad, Glad, Afraid, Ashamed, Hurt.

Our immediate purpose is to discover and identify in order to see clearly who I am and what needs change. Acceptance of *what is* precedes change. Seeing and accepting *what is* is very difficult, however, because we don't know that we don't know. We are in many ways blind and self-deluded, but we insist that: "I know who I am and where I'm going," or "I know what's best for me." We are deluded and don't know it. In fact, most of us deny it. This is what allows us to fall back into the same destructive behaviors again, not having learned anything from the last one. How many times has a friend or relative said: "I saw you building up to it, but you insisted everything was OK!" The assumption that self-delusion is a fact is basic to group therapy.

The way we illustrate this self-delusion is with the Johari Window:

MYSELF

OTHERS

1 OPEN	2 SECRET
3 BLIND	4 SUBCONSCIOUS

The window's four panes represent four aspects of our total self. As the diagram indicates, only the top two panes are visible to myself. Nos. 3 and 4 are hidden from my view. This is descriptive of the self-delusion that keeps me from seeing what I'm *really* like and allows my slow disintegration to continue with only a slight, if any, recognition on my part of how bad things have become. A more accurate picture of myself is essential to recovery.

Window No. 1 is open. This is visible to "Self" and to "Others" and contains material I am willing to share with you—my interests, vocation, and virtues, to name a few. This is open information about myself.

Window No. 2 is secret. I know things about me that I don't want you to know. I fear the loss of esteem if you see me as having such feelings as hostility, suspicion, inferiority, resentment, or self-pity. Revealing these feelings is called *leveling.* I level with you when I take the risk of letting you really know me by spontaneously reporting my feelings. Leveling is one of the two most important techniques in self-discovery.

We are blind to Window No. 3, and yet it is seen by others. The tone of our voice, the tilt of our head, tell others things about us that we don't see. Many times a perfect stranger can see more in us in half an hour than we have discovered in years of self-examination. When someone tells us how we appear to them, they are *confronting* us. Confrontation is the second vital technique in breaking through self-delusion to self-discovery.

The existence of the large blind area illustrated by Window No. 3 means that we are dependent on others taking the risk of confronting us with this material if we are to ever come to know it. "It takes at least 2 to know 1."

Window No. 4 is subconscious and not visible. While leveling and confronting often result in a glimpse into the unconscious, this is a bonus and not a goal of group therapy.

Confrontation

It takes courage to risk confronting. We have all traded our honesty for the approval of others in the past. However, if we care about our fellow group members, and if we want them to be honest with us in return, we will present them with our picture of them.

Confrontation is defined as: *presenting a person with himself by describing how I see him.* Confrontation is most useful when spoken with concern and accompanied with examples of the confronted behavior or *data.*

"You seem self-centered to me because you only talk about yourself. . . ."

"You seem hostile because of the sarcastic answers you give. . . ."

"Your voice sounds so sad I see you feeling sorry for yourself. . . ."

"Your face is so red you seem very angry . . ."

"John, each time Joe confronts you, you explain yourself instead of leveling with him. How do you *feel* about what Joe told you?"

or

"John, you go into a long silence after each confrontation instead of leveling. How are you feeling when you withdraw in silence?"

For the most part defenses, including attitudinal postures, are unintentional and automatic shields against a real or imagined threat to our self-esteem. By pointing out the defenses we are using, we are given a better chance of letting down this wall that is locking others out and keeping us prisoners. For this blocks our getting close to others as well as getting closer to ourselves. Coming to recognize these blocks to self-discovery may enable us to look behind them to discover the feelings concealed from view. Long explanations may hide feelings of inadequacy and guilt. Since defenses and attitudinal postures do hide us from ourselves as well as others, it is important to identify them. A lot of this is new, so while you are getting used to it, just *trust your impulses.* Spontaneous expressions tend to be much more honest. It is more helpful to be *revealing* than to be *right.*

Most of us tend to think we already know ourselves and are afraid of looking bad, so it is hard for us to take the risk of being revealing and genuine. But what have we really got to lose? Remember how unsuccessful our previous attempts to change have been? Since we can't change something until we really see it and accept its existence, we should ask ourselves: "Do I really accept something if I keep it a secret?" Risking openness is the key. When you are tempted to withdraw into silence, remember that we are all in the same boat, and a common feeling of everyone when he is introduced to the group is *fear.*

Frequently, in place of confronting a person with some data that we have observed (what they said—how they look, or sound, etc.) we make the mistake of guessing—of asking questions.

"I bet you fight a lot with your wife."

"Did your parents raise you very strictly. . . ?"

A guess or a question is not confrontation.

Another mistake is advice-giving in place of confronting:

"Don't let people walk all over you so much . . ." To state this as confrontation would be:

"You seem like a doormat, the way you let people walk all over you." This way we are not playing God by advising, but we are letting the person see himself from another point of view and trusting him to seek advice if he wants it.

Confrontation is descriptive of what we have observed in the person we are confronting. Guesses, advice, or discussions about something we have not witnessed is not confrontation. In a sense, when we confront, we hold up a mirror to let another person know how he appears to us.

We are most useful as confronters when we are not so much trying to change another person as we are trying to help him see himself more accurately. Change, if it comes, comes later when the person chooses it and enlists the spiritual help that the Sixth and Seventh Steps of the AA Program describe.

Picture a gardener preparing a proper environment within the soil so that the seeds he plants may receive the gift of *growth* from a Power greater than himself. Imagine a physician cleaning a wound to provide an environment to receive the gift of *healing.* The change we are all seeking might be more correctly labeled *healing* or *growth,* and while it is largely a gift of a Power greater than ourselves, the necessary environment for the gift is an honest picture of who and what we are like now. Because of our egocentric *blindness* and self-delusion, we are *all* dependent on others for that completed picture. Confrontation provides it.

Leveling

To respond openly to being confronted is to *level.* We *level* when we take the risk of being known by spontaneously reporting our feelings. For example: We *level* when we let someone know we are hurt—or afraid—or angry.

Using these feelings as an example of leveling is probably useful for two reasons. Anger bottled up, or fear that is kept hidden, seem to lead to more relapses than any other feelings. Also, anger and fear (along with affection) are usually the hardest feelings for us to report. Frequently, people make the mistake of assuming that the purpose of group therapy is to make someone angry. Anger is an important feeling. But it is only one feeling among many that we want to discover and level with.

If, instead of leveling, we respond without naming a feeling, we are hiding. The ways we hide our feelings are many, and we call them *defenses.* Each defense serves to avoid naming the feelings we are *now* experiencing. This prevents us from being known. One of the most helpful things that the group can do is to help a member identify his defenses.

Defenses which we all use to some extent are:

Rationalizing	Minimizing
Justifying	Evading, dodging
Projecting	Defiance
Blaming, accusing	Attacking, aggression
Judging, moralizing	Withdrawing
Intellectualizing	Silence
Analyzing	Verbalizing, talking
Explaining	Shouting, intimidating
Theorizing	Threatening
Generalizing	Frowning
Quibbling, equivocating	Glaring
Debating, arguing	Staring
Sparring	Joking
Questioning, interrogating	Grinning, smiling, laughing
Switching	Projecting
Denying	Agreeing
Being smug, superior, or arrogant	Complying

Try leveling with that feeling of fear for a starter and discover how that makes you feel. You'll probably find, as others have, that when you report a feeling you modify and reduce it. Keeping it a secret seems to increase its power. If we don't begin now to risk being genuine and self-revealing, when will we ever really do it?

Appendix C

PATIENT'S SELF-EVALUATION

ALCOHOLISM REHABILITATION PROGRAM

Filled in by patient, then put in patient's chart.

Biographical Profile

(The information that you present here will serve as a basis for helping us to get to know and serve you better and will be kept in the strictest professional confidence.)

Mr., Mrs., Miss________Occupation________Date ________________

Address (street, city, state) ______________________________

Phone______Birth date______Age______Place of birth ________________

Ethnic background (Irish, English, French, etc.) ________________

____

Religious background________________________________

What do you expect from this place? ________________________

____

When and how did your difficulties begin?______________________

____

To what do you attribute the cause of your problem? ____________

How do your difficulties affect you emotionally and physically?________

____

How do they affect others? ______________________________

Describe any previous psychiatric contacts and experiences____________

____

What earlier problems are still with you? _____________________

Which have been solved, and how did you solve them? _____________

____

How could life have been different?_________________________

Health

Height_____Weight_____List any physical handicaps ____________________
Identifying physical characteristics ______________________________
Childhood illnesses, surgery, or accidents ________________________
Adult illnesses (give dates) ____________________________________

Describe any medication presently taking ________________________

Financial

Type of residence________How long________Mortgage $ ______________
Describe your car____________ How much life insurance do you/spouse carry $ ____________
Additional sources of income besides job ________________________
Last year's total family incomes______ Total debts______ Yearly living expenses________

Interests

Hobbies and leisure activities __________________________________

Books and magazines read in past 6 months ________________________

Social and professional organizations and clubs (with offices held). Include past and present and circle those presently active:

What is your idea of a "good time"? _____________________________
Liquor preferences ____
What are your plans for the future? _____________________________

In what additional activities would you like to engage now? ____________

Work History

Job Description	Dates Start—Finish	Reason for leaving	Earnings
1.			
2.			
3.			
4.			
5.			

Explain ever being fired or discharged________________

List any other job held (include part-time)________________

What are your strongest qualities as an employee ________________

Military

Branch military service (if deferred or 4-F, explain) ________________
Military duties________________
Rank at discharge________Type of discharge ________________

Education

Highest school grade completed______Age completed______rank __________
College attended (with dates)________Major subjects __________
Degrees (with dates)________Extra curricular activities, organizations, and offices held:

Special educational training or courses (with dates) ________________

Family Background

Age of father______of mother______(if either parent is ill, describe illness; if deceased, give date and cause) ________________

By whom were you raised?________Describe your childhood ______________
____

Describe your mother as you remember her ______________
In what ways are you like her? ______________
Describe your father as you remember him ______________
To whom did you feel closest and why? ______________
To whom did you go for help with personal problems and why? ______________
____

Ages and occupations of brothers ______________
Ages and occupations of sisters ______________

Marital

Single	Marriage plans	Date married	Date separated	Date divorced	Date remarried	Date widowed

Names/ages of children ______________
Describe your children ______________
____

Spouse's age______Describe your spouse (use adjectives) ______________
____

Spouse's occupation ______________
Describe yourself ______________
What are your main strengths?______________
What do you or others regard as your shortcomings? ______________
____

Drinking Behavior

When were you first concerned about drinking?________Why? ______________
____

Age when you had your first drink ______________
Age when you first lost control of drinking ______________
Age when you had your first blackout ______________
Age when your blackouts began to increase ______________
Have you ever been arrested? ______________
What was/were the reason(s)? ______________
Have you been drinking alone?______________
Were you ever treated in a mental hospital? ______________

Were you ever treated for problem drinking? ______

Age you first drank "the morning after" ______

Age when you tried first to change your drinking pattern, i.e., rules, pledges, etc. ______

What effect does your drinking have on your job and/or social life? ______

Do your attitudes change when you drink? ______

Have your family activities changed because of your drinking? ______

Has your sexual life changed because of your drinking? ______

Have you ever been on a binge or bender? ______

Have you ever used substitutes for alcoholic beverages, such as mouthwash, hair tonic, etc.? ______

Have you ever used barbiturates, tranquilizers, sleeping pills, etc.? ______

Have you ever had convulsions, hallucinations, DT.'s? ______

Does it take more or less alcohol to get relief than it used to five years ago? ______

Have you needed to continue drinking so you wouldn't have the shakes or other uncomfortable symptoms? ______

When did you have your last drink? ______

How many times have you been on the wagon in the last two (2) years? ______

What is your longest period of sobriety in:

a. the past two years? ______

b. the past five years? ______

Have you had any treatment for problem drinking or drug problems before? Please give dates ______

Have you ever joined AA? ______

How many meetings have you attended? ______

Feelings about Drinking

	Yes	No	
1.	___	___	Have you changed your drinking place or friends in the last few years? Is there more drinking now?
2.	___	___	Do you drink because you have problems?
3.	___	___	Do you get vexed when your spouse or friend tells you you are drinking too much?
4.	___	___	Do you forget something you did when drinking?
5.	___	___	Do you ever do anything when drinking that you are ashamed of?

6. ___ ___ Do you ever go "on the wagon" or just stick to beer so you won't get too drunk?
7. ___ ___ Do you feel you can hold your drinks better than your friends?
8. ___ ___ Do you look forward to times when you can drink?
9. ___ ___ Do you stay away from people who don't drink?
10. ___ ___ Do you avoid any talk about the disease of alcoholism?
11. ___ ___ Do you tell yourself that others drink more than you? That drinking has never caused you any trouble?
12. ___ ___ Do you ever drink more than you planned to? Or get drunk when you didn't want to?

Appendix D

COUNSELOR'S INITIAL INTERVIEW

CHEMICAL DEPENDENCY CENTER

Name ______________________ Admission date ________
(Last) (First) (Middle)
Residence ______________________ Case number ________
Age __ Marital Status S M W D No. of children ________ Age range ____ church ______
Occupation ______________________ Educ. ________

I. PRESENT ILLNESS:

A. Motivation

1. What led up to your coming here?

2. Why are you here? (If exposed to treatment before, what do you feel we can do for you at this time?)

3. How do you feel about your drinking?

II. INSIGHT:

A. Self

1. Do you think your drinking is different from that of social drinkers? If so, in what way?

2. When did you first notice you were drinking differently than you'd like to?

3. Does your behavior generally change when drinking (in relation to family, co-workers, and associates)? If so, in what way?

B. Family:

1. When you were a child, what was your father's attitude toward drinking?

Case Number______

2. When you were a child, what was your mother's attitude toward drinking?

3. What is your spouse's attitude toward drinking?

4. Were you closer to your father, mother, or neither?

5. Is there anyone who knows how you really feel inside?

6. Are you satisfied with the way your family is treating you? If not, why?

7. Do you think your spouse will participate in your treatment here? Should she?

III. SOBRIETY HISTORY:

A. Former treatment of problem? When was this?

B. What is the longest period you've gone without a drink outside of a hospital or institution? When was this?

C. Why did you stop drinking for that period?

D. How were you able to do this?

IV. DRUG PATTERNS:

A. Do you take any kind of pills or medication for your nerves or sleep, prescribed or otherwise?
Explain—i.e., name of pill and length of time used.

B. Do you feel the medication is helpful?

C. Do you always take it as the doctor ordered?

V. EFFORTS MADE TO HELP SELF:

A. Did you ever join AA? When:
Where: Regularity:

Case Number______

B. What part of the AA program seems to be the most helpful to you?

C. What part of the AA program seems to give you the most difficulty?

D. Have you ever had an AA sponsor?
Name and address:

E. What ways or means have you used to stay away from drinking?

VI. MILITARY SERVICE:

A. Were you in the service? If not, why not?
Type of discharge:

B. Service connected disability or pension?

C. Ever disciplined in service? Explain:

VII. SELF-EVALUATION:

A. How serious do you think your problem really is?

B. What reasons would you give yourself for not drinking?

C. Any questions you would like to ask me?

D. (If patient brings up length of stay) Do you foresee anything that may interfere with your completing treatment here?

IX. COUNSELOR'S IMPRESSION: (date)

Appendix E

MEANINGFUL PERSON EVALUATION FORM

Filled in by the spouse or some family member, returned to unit and placed in patient's chart.

Patient's Case Number: ________

Date: ____________________

Full Name: ____________________

Address: ____________________

Telephone: ____________________ Age: ______

What is your occupation? (Check one)

____Housewife

____Laborer (Construction, Cleaning, Stock Work, etc.)

____Trained Worker (Carpenter, Bus Driver, Secretary, etc.)

____Supervisor (Foreman, Office Manager, etc.)

____Own Small Business (Farm, Restaurant, Barbershop, etc.)

____Sales (Real Estate, Stock, Cars, etc.)

____Business Executive

____Professional (Teacher, Lawyer, Engineer, Doctor, etc.)

____Unemployed—No Occupation

____Other—Specify ____________

____

Patient Number______

Instructions:

Indicate the answers to the following questions by placing a check _✓ in the blank next to the response you choose or by writing in the space provided.

Confidential

Relationship to the Patient

1. What is your relationship to the patient?

___Spouse ___ Sibling
___Parent ___ Other relative
___Child ___ Friend
___Other

2. How many years has this relationship existed?

___Less than a year
___One to two years
___Three to five years
___Six to ten years
___More than ten years

3. Are you living with the patient at the present time?

___Yes
___No

4. Do you intend to continue living with the patient?

___Yes
___No
___Uncertain

Questions 5 through 8 are for spouses only.

5. How many times have you been married?

___Once
___Twice
___Three times
___More than three times

6. How many times have you and the patient been separated and lived apart?

___Once ___ More than three
___Twice ___ None
___Three times

7. How long was your longest period of separation?

___More than a week but less than a month
___More than a month but less than three months
___Four to six months
___Seven months to a year
___Longer than a year
___Never separated

8. Would you consider this a happy marriage, except for the drinking?

___Yes
___No
___Uncertain

9. How many male children does the patient have (from all marriages)?___ List their approximate ages here and circle the ones who presently live with the patient or his spouse:

____

10. How many female children does the patient have (from all marriages)? ___List their approximate ages here

Patient Number______

and circle the ones who presently live with the patient or his spouse:

____

Questions 11, 12, and 13 concern minor children only.

11. Are any of the children living with the patient or his spouse difficult to discipline or do they show other behavior problems?

___Yes
___No
___Uncertain

Comments: ______________________

12. Do any of the children seem to have personality or emotional problems?

___Yes
___No

Comments: ______________________

____

13. Do any of the children seem to have difficulties or problems in school?

___Yes
___No
___Uncertain

Comments: ______________________

____

14. Is any family member besides the patient presently receiving professional help for personality, emotional, or behavior problems?

___Yes
___No
___Uncertain

15. If so, please name the family member or members here: ____________

____

16. From whom is this help being received?

____

____

17. Do any family members other than the patient drink to excess?

___Yes
___No

If so, name the family members here:

____

If you are the patient's spouse or are another concerned person who is presently living with the patient, it is essential that you answer questions 18 through 34. If not, skip to question 35.

19. I suffer from fears and anxieties a lot of the time.

___True
___False

20. I often feel insecure.

___True
___False

21. I feel that I love the patient deeply.

___True
___False

22. Children often annoy and anger me.

___True
___False

23. When someone I know is ill or in trouble, I nearly always feel I must help them until they are well or the trouble is over.

___True
___False

24. I have rarely felt angry, hostile, or resentful toward the patient.

___True

Patient Number______

___False

25. I think drinking alcoholic beverages is disgusting even for nonalcoholics.

___True

___False

26. I feel that the patient loves me deeply.

___True

___False

27. I have had serious personality or emotional problems in the past.

___True

___False

28. I presently have serious personality or emotional problems.

___True

___False

29. If the above is true, are you receiving professional help?

___Yes

___No

30. From whom are you receiving this help?

___Do not wish to say

___Medical doctor

___Psychiatrist

___Psychologist

___Clergyman

___Social worker

___Friend

___Other

31. My use of alcoholic beverages is best characterized as:

___Never

___A problem to me

___Something I use to relax

___Normal social drinking

32. Others have told me that I drink too much.

___True

___False

33. I presently am taking:

___Tranquilizers

___Diet pills or pep pills

___Neither

34. I have on occasion used marijuana.

___True

___False

35. I feel that the patient should quit drinking out of love for me.

___True

___False

All concerned persons and spouse should answer the remaining questions.

36. I have at times drunk to excess with the patient.

___True

___False

37. I have gone on drinking parties with the patient in the past.

___True

___False

38. I feel responsible for the patient's drinking.

___Not at all

___Some

___Very much

39. I sometimes feel guilty about the patient's drinking.

___True

___False

40. I feel that the patient could quit drinking if he wanted to badly enough.

___True

Patient Number______

___False

41. The patient simply lacks the will power to quit drinking.

___True

___False

42. Alcoholism is not a disease so much as it is a sin and a moral problem.

___True

___False

43. I feel the patient isn't really an alcoholic but rather has a drinking problem.

___True

___False

44. I feel that if the treatment is successful, the patient will be able to return to normal social drinking.

___True

___False

45. I have tried in the past to make the patient quit drinking.

___True

___False

Patient's Drinking History

46. How long has the patient been drinking heavily?

___6 months or less

___6 months to a year

___Between 1 and 2 years

___Between 2 and 3 years

___At least 5 years

___More than 10 years

47. How many years altogether has the patient been drinking?

___1 year

___2 years

___3 years

___4 years

___5–10 years

___10–15 years

___more than 15 years

48. Has the patient's drinking interfered with his marriage in the past?

___Yes

___No

___Not applicable as patient has never married

49. Has the patient's drinking interfered with his social relations with friends?

___Yes

___No

How? ________________________

____

50. Has the patient's drinking had a bad effect on his financial condition?

___Yes

___No

How? ________________________

____

51. Has the patient's drinking damaged his health?

___Yes

___No

If so, please tell us how his health is damaged. ____________________

____

52. How many times in his lifetime has the patient previously been hospitalized for any reason?

___None	___ 4
___1	___ 5
___2	___ More than 5
___3	

Patient Number______

53. How many times has the patient been previously hospitalized or been in a treatment center for alcoholism or other chemical dependency?

___None
___1
___2
___3
___ 4
___ 5
___ More than 5

54. Has the patient ever been arrested for reckless driving or for speeding?

___Yes
___No

Dates: ____________________

55. Has the patient ever been arrested for driving while intoxicated?

___Yes
___No

Dates: ____________________

56. Has the patient ever been arrested for drunken and disorderly conduct?

___Yes
___No

Dates: ____________________

57. Has the patient ever been arrested for assaultive behavior?

___Yes
___No

Dates: ____________________

58. When the patient gets drunk, does he tend to get abusive to others?

___Yes
___No

Describe ____________________

____

59. Has the patient ever beat up members of his family?

___Yes
___No

Explain ____________________

____

60. Has the patient ever been arrested for bad checks?

___Yes
___No

Dates ____________________

61. Does the patient have any outstanding loans other than a car or house loan?

___Yes
___No

Describe ____________________

____

62. Has the patient ever taken out a loan and used most of the money to buy liquor and/or drugs?

___Yes
___No

63. Has the patient ever placed any of his or his family's belongings "in hock" in order to obtain money to purchase liquor and/or drugs?

___Yes
___No

64. Does the patient feel resentful toward you right now?

___Yes
___No

65. Did the patient just prior to treatment use tranquilizers, pep pills, or diet pills?

___Yes
___No

66. Has the patient used marijuana?

___No
___Yes, tried it
___Yes, uses it frequently

Patient Number_____

67. Does the patient use large quantities of cough syrup or other liquid drugs which may contain codeine?
___No
___Yes, but only for medical reasons
___Yes, uses it frequently for non-medical reasons

68. Does the patient sneak drinks on the sly?
___Yes
___No
Describe ____________________

69. Does the patient engage in binge drinking?
___Yes
___No
Describe ____________________

70. Has the patient told lies about drinking?
___Yes
___No
Describe ____________________

71. Is the patient sometimes preoccupied with drinking?
___Yes
___No
Describe ____________________

72. Has the patient shown any sudden personality changes?
___Yes
___No
Describe ____________________

73. Has the patient ever had a faulty memory as a result of drinking?
___Yes
___No
Describe ____________________

74. Has the patient ever had a convulsion?
___Yes
___No

75. Has the patient ever had hallucinations?
___Yes
___No

76. Does the patient usually drink alone or with others?
___Alone
___With others

77. Does the patient drink to ease tensions?
___Yes
___No
Describe ____________________

78. When the patient drinks, does he gulp drinks or drink unusually fast?
___Yes
___No
Describe ____________________

79. Have you noticed any periods when the patient has suddenly increased or decreased his amount of drinking?
___Yes
___No

80. Does the patient hide bottles?
___Yes
___No

Patient Number______

Describe ________________________
____

81. Does the patient drink to relieve fatigue?
___Yes
___No
Describe ________________________
____

82. Has the patient ever had tremors in the morning after rising?
___Yes
___No

83. Does the patient have times when he must drink and will go to great lengths to get a drink?
___Yes
___No
Describe ________________________
____

84. Does the patient drink in the morning?
___Yes
___No

Patient's Employment History

85. How many jobs has the patient had in the last two yeas?
___None (has been unemployed)
___1 ___ 2
___3 ___ 4
___More than 4

86. If the patient is unemployed, how long has he been unemployed?
___From 0 to 6 months
___6 months to a year
___1 to 2 years
___2 to 5 years
___More than 5 years

87. How long was the patient employed on his last job?
___Less than a month
___From 1 to 6 months
___6 months to a year
___1 to 2 years
___2 to 5 years
___More than 5 years

88. What is the longest period of time the patient has held the same job?
___A few weeks
___A few months (less than a year)
___1 to 2 years
___3 to 5 years
___5 to 10 years
___More than 10 years

89. Within the last year, has the patient had any accident while on the job?
___Yes
___No

90. While on his most recent job, was the patient frequently absent or out on sick leave?
___Yes
___No
Describe ________________________
____

91. On his last job, was the patient frequently tardy?
___Yes
___No

92. Did the patient, while on his last job, begin to withdraw from relationships with his fellow co-workers?
___Yes
___No
Describe ________________________

Patient Number______

93. Was the patient's efficiency and productivity on his most recent job affected by his drinking?
___Yes
___No
Describe ______________________________
____

94. How much income has this patient received in the last 6 months from employment only?
___None
___Less than $500
___$500 to $1000
___$1000 to $2000
___More than $2000

Appendix F

FIRST STEP PREPARATION

Instructions:

Each patient on the Chemical Dependency Unit is required to make a list of destructive behaviors caused by his or her

1. powerlessness over mood-altering chemicals.
2. unmanageable life.

This step cannot be overemphasized, because until each one of us accepts the seriousness and totality of this illness, no treatment or recovery is possible. Some guidelines for writing out this step are outlined below.

A. Examples of powerlessness over mood-altering chemicals are:
   1. kinds, amounts, and frequency
   2. loss of memory and blackouts while intoxicated
   3. destructive behavior
   4. accidents caused and dangerous situations produced
   5. preoccupation
   6. attempts to control alcohol and/or drugs

B. Examples of unmanageability (even when not using or under the influence of chemicals):
   1. physical or medical condition
   2. emotional or feeling life
   3. social and family life
   4. spiritual life
   5. occupational

Appendix G

OUTPATIENT'S HANDBOOK

ENCOUNTER GROUP

Goals

1. Immediate goal: Discovery of feelings / defences in ourselves and in others.

Discovery (uncovering) of feelings and defenses, to come to an awareness (insight, recognition, knowledge, understanding) of them. N.B.—We assist each other in *discovering* feelings and defenses, in achieving awareness of them. We do not pass judgment on them or try to change them for each other.

2. Ultimate goal: Accurate empathy—that is, a sensitiveness to (awareness of, insight into, recognition of) the feelings of others which enables us to choose spontaneously (readily, quickly) the most appropriate behavior responses in communication with others.

   Accurate empathy—A sensitiveness to the feelings of others which enables us to achieve comfortable interpersonal relations (comfortable for ourselves and for others).

Ground Rules

1. Our focus is *here and now.* Therefore, not past history, episodes, experiences, problems, and not future plans, hopes, intentions, resolutions, expectations, possibilities.
2. Our focus is *feeling* here and now. Therefore, not ideas, analyses, opinions, judgments (moral or analytic), guesses, discussions, debates, speculations.
3. Our focus is *defenses* here and now. Therefore, not "game-playing," maneuvering, sparring, moralizing, competing, contesting.
4. We stick to *data* here and now. Data are factual evidence as it appears to the members of the group. There are two sources of here and now data:

a. Content: what is said (stated, presented, told).
For example: "I feel angry."

b. Process: how it is said (the manner, mode, behavior which accompanies or goes along with the statement.
For example: flushed face, flashing eyes, aggressive voice, clenched fists.

5. In encountering each other, we use two means:
   a. *Leveling*—that is, I tell you (reveal to you, inform you) how I feel (what I am feeling here and now).
   b. *Confronting*—that is, I tell you (inform you, reveal to you) how you appear to me to be feeling here and now.

In both leveling and confronting we make simple, direct statements of fact, providing only as many data as are necessary to support (confirm, make evident, clear) our statement.

For example, when I level:
"I feel angry" (statement of fact). +Content+
"I am tense. My face feels hot. I seem to be boiling inside." (Data) +Process+

For example, when I confront:
"You appear to feel angry" (statement of fact).
"You appear tense. Your face is red. Your eyes are flashing. Your fists are clenched. Your voice is harsh." (Data)

Feelings (Emotions)

Feelings are a common endowment of our human nature. We all have them; and we all experience the same feelings. Feelings, therefore, are a common ground for relating and communicating with other people. When I am aware of my feelings and yours, I am in a position to respond appropriately toward you, having regard for your feelings. This works both ways. If I am unaware of my feelings and yours, I am not in a postition to respond appropriately. This works both ways, too. Awareness of feelings, therefore, is essential for appropriate feeling responses.

Feelings, of course, are not the only endowment of our human nature; they are not the only common ground for relating and communicating with others. We all have intellects, imaginations, memories, wills, and physical powers. We can relate and communicate with ideas, fantasies, recollections, shared love, choices and actions, physical contacts, and expressions. However, our focus is on feelings, not on the other powers or means of relating and communicating.

We are, in effect, a "laboratory" for growth in feeling awareness during our regular encounter group sessions.

Why focus on feelings? For several reasons—

1. We are all "phony"—to some extent. To be phony means to be false, dishonest, inconsistent, misleading, deceptive with ourselves and with others. How does this happen?

Repression is one common way of becoming phony. We all have some feelings we don't like. They are uncomfortable, unpleasant, unwelcome, so we try to avoid them. One way to avoid them (temporarily) is to repress them, to shove them aside, tuck them out of sight, disregard, ignore, hide them, conceal them —we repress them and *pretend we don't have them.* (That's phony!)

On the other hand, there are some feelings we all like. They are comfortable, pleasant, welcome, etc., so *we pretend we have them.* (That's phony, too.)

We become double-phonies, pretending we don't have certain feelings and pretending we do have certain other feelings. Take some examples. What feelings do you like? What feelings do you dislike?

In addition to the fact that we all like and dislike some feelings, there are moralistic taboos and approvals placed on certain feelings. Some feelings are "no-no's"; others are "yes-yeses." We are told (and we tell ourselves) that we *shouldn't* have some feelings and we *should* have others. As a result, we strive not to have the "no-no" feelings and we try always to have the "yes-yeses."

It doesn't work, of course. When we do experience the "no-no" feelings, we feel *guilty;* we label ourselves "bad," we experience remorse, lose self-esteem, feel unworthy, despise and reject ourselves. And we expect these same reactions from others. We're "in a bag." This is an extremely distasteful situation, so we pretend we don't have those "no-no" feelings. (This is phony.)

On the other hand, we give moralistic approval to "yes-yes" feelings. So we pretend always to have them. (This is phony.) We are now double-phony compounded.

Take some examples . . . What are your "no-no" feelings? What are your "yes-yes" feelings?

A necessary condition for discovering feelings (and defenses) and developing accurate empathy is to regard feelings as *facts* and to accept them as present in ourselves and others whether we like them or not and without moralistic labels of "good" or "bad."

2. Another reason for focusing on feelings is the fact that ordinarily we do not do so. We discuss ideas, intellectualize, analyze problems, express opinions, exchange fantasies and memories, play golf, bridge or poker, have some physical contact with each other—but for the most part, we ignore or shove aside our feelings. We actually lose awareness of our own (and others') feelings. We not

only don't, we *cannot* relate and communicate with others on a feeling level. We simply don't know how. We build defenses to protect and hide our feelings; we assume positions, often fixed and rigid, in regard to feelings. They are "out of bounds" for most of us, and our defenses are barriers between us. Yet until I know your feelings and you know mine, we don't know each other; we can't, because so large and significant a part of us lies hidden from view. If we don't know each other, we fear each other, we mistrust each other. We don't know what to expect of each other, so we remain constantly on guard, defensive, wary, cautious, distant. We live as strangers, even as enemies, to each other.

In an encounter group we do not deny, "put down," or minimize our intellect and other powers; we deliberately take the focus away from them and direct it to feelings for a while.

3. Feelings are here and now. All of us *have* feelings—here and now. We are interacting with each other constantly on the feeling level. Therefore we have a common ground for relating and communicating, regardless of our differences in age, education, socioeconomic status, political and moral values, intellectual opinions and prejudices, physical abilities or disabilities.

Since feelings operate here and now, we have a common pool of immediate, existential data with which to deal. We are all actually participating in a shared experience. By directing our attention to this, we need not burden our relations and communications with the past or the future, or with problems and experiences which are out side of this room and are therefore not common to and experienced by all of us together here and now.

It will be helpful to agree on some broad classifications of categories of feelings as a framework for learning to identify them. Each category includes a wide spectrum of feelings, varying greatly in intensity.

Pursuit Feelings	*Avoidance Feelings*
Ordinary	
Love (a feeling of attraction toward "good")	*Hate* (a feeling of revulsion against "evil")
Liking of	Dislike of
Warmth toward	Cold toward
Affection for	Indifferent to
Passion for	Repelled by
Tenderness toward	Despise
Drawn toward	Withdrawn from
Friendly toward	
Captivated by	
Concern for	

Admiration for
Wonder at
Attracted by

Desire (a feeling of movement toward, in the direction of, a "good" which is loved)
Longing for
Craving for
Coveting
Need for
Impulse toward
Impelled toward
Hanker for
Want
Curious
Inquisitive
Nosey

Aversion (a feeling of movement away from an "evil" which is hated)
Turn away from
Withdrawn from
Rejection of
Distant from
Repelled by
Get out, get away from
Escape
Avoid
Evade

Hope (a feeling of confident expectation that the "good" we love and desire will be ours—will be achieved or possessed by whatever help is needed)
Expectant of
Anticipate
Aspire to
Trust
Reliance on
"Faith" in
Buoyancy
Brightness
Confidence

Despair (a feeling of expectation of "evil"; of expectation that a "good" which is loved and desired cannot and will not be attained—or, that an "evil" which is hated cannot or will not be avoided)
Hopeless
Desperate
Inevitable
Despondent
Doubtful
Skeptical
Suspicious
Discouraged
Disappointment
Trapped
Cornered
Stopped
Defeated
Helpless
Inadequate
Lost

Joy (a feeling of delight which accompanies the achieving or possession of a "good")
Happy
Pleased/pleasant

Sorrow (a feeling of sadness which accompanies the loss of a "good" or the presence of an "evil")
Sad—saddened
Grieved
Embarrassed
Humilated

Satisfied
Refreshed
Completed
Fulfilled
Gratified
Gleeful
Delighted
Calm
Peaceful
Tranquil
Relieved
Comfortable
Contented

Depressed
Melancholy
Unhappy
Sorry
Pity
Dejected
Gloomy
Dour
Hurt
Wounded
Martyred
Ashamed
Crushed

Overwhelmed
Put down
Rejected
Humbled
Disgusted

Emergency

Courage (a feeling of strength to overcome difficulties in the way of achieving a "good" or enduring an "evil")

Spunk
Guts
Bravery
Risking
Patience
Endurance
Toughness
Confidence
Competence
Assurance
Bold
Audacious
Cocky

Fear (a feeling of dread in the presence of or from the threat of danger

Terror
Panic
Alarm
Trepidation
Horror
Timid
Fright
Scare
Anxiety
Nervousness
Jumpy
Jittery
Appalled
Apprehension
Worry

Flight
Escape
Uneasy
Restless
Cowed
Cowardly
Cautious
Distrust
Mistrust
Astonished
Startled

Anger (a feeling of strong antagonism, displeasure toward an "evil" difficult to avoid or an "evil" which blocks the attaining of good)

Fury
Rage
Ire

Resentment
Mad
Grouchy

Indignation	Grumpy
Wrath	Disgruntled
Irritation	Bugged
Annoyance	Aggravated
Belligerence	
Hostility	

Appendix H

HOSPITAL PERSONNEL TRAINING HANDBOOK

EXAMPLE OF 4-DAY PERSONNEL TRAINING SESSION

Second, as we live together learning to use both sets of data we provide each other in communication—*content* and *process,*—and endeavoring to be more and more open with each other, we will come to see and to know ourselves more completely through others' eyes. As we achieve increased life of conscious interdependence, we will not only see others more accurately and completely as persons, but—more important—see ourselves as persons as well.

I am to be your guide in this experience, bringing whatever theory, based on clinical insights and controlled social experiments, may apply from time to time during the week.

Our schedule will have three basic elements: the E Group, where there will be no designated leader, but where we can find out more clearly what we communicate to other people; the *Simulation* of actual counseling and other encounters with alcoholics; and finally a *Syndetic Session,* where we will try to tie together loose ends and have a bull session on what does or does not make sense.

Communication I

There are two kinds of data in communication, namely:

1. Content—the words we say.
2. Process—how we say it (tones, inflections, flushed faces, expression in eyes, etc.). This is the message we send and receive around the words.

ENCOUNTER

Leveling is presenting the other person with myself at a feeling level. *Confronting* is presenting the other person with himself as I see him in this encounter.

Opening Session

I. Purpose of session and overview.
—to help us get into our work rapidly and efficiently
—presentation on how we got here
—what we are up to
—how we will go about it

II. Presentation of workshop purpose.
—to help us discover ourselves as persons and to increase our skills in working with alcoholism individually, socially, and religiously.

III. How do we go about it?

1. In exploration group
—by experiencing and reflecting in face-to-face meeting, with reflection on the meeting
—by speaking to actual data
—by focusing primarily on the here and now
—by expecting a difference between this and other groups

2. By other types of educational experiences

Our exploration group may be different from the learning experience you expected. Essentially, it is an effort to combine two goals in one by using the laboratory method. In face-to-face encounter we will examine our own and other members' defense systems, and examine our own abilities to empathize with others' circumstances and situations and to confront them as the need and proper time arise. At the same time, we shall be learning these as skills necessary to counseling alcoholics and their families. The practice these experiences provide will improve our ability to meet the problems of the alcoholics in our hospitals and communities.

A. Timing (when receivable and useful)
B. Supportive (nonthreatening)
C. Specific (descriptive of actual behavior)
D. "Speaking the truth in love"

Communication II

1. We think it looks like

2. But because of other factors not taken into account actually there is an arc of distortion.

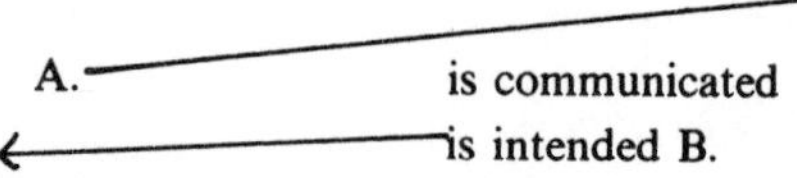

3. Six things at least are present.
   a. I say
   b. I think I say
   c. You hear
   d. You think you hear
   e. What you think you hear
   f. What you think I think you hear

DISTORTION

1. There are two types of factors which distort.

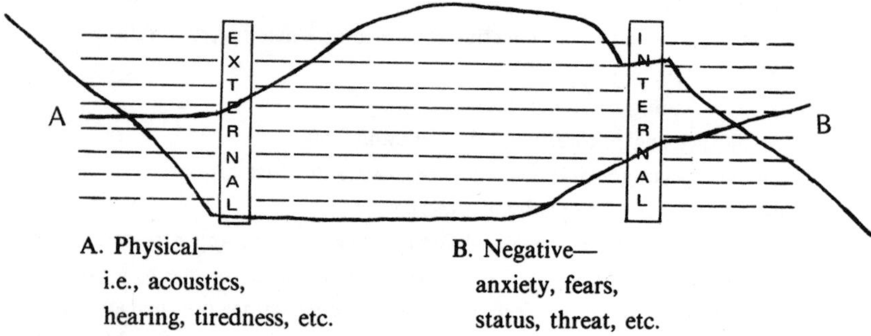

A. Physical—
i.e., acoustics,
hearing, tiredness, etc.

B. Negative—
anxiety, fears,
status, threat, etc.

a. Circular Process of Social Interaction

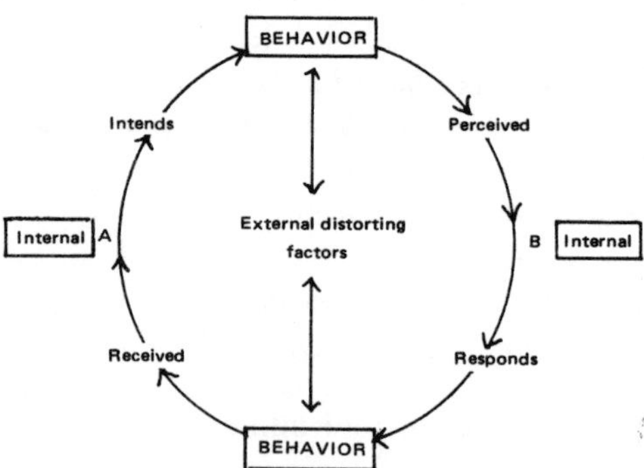

As A acts, his message is filtered 3 times—within himself, externally, and within B—then 3 times more from B back to A.

Feedback lets a person know how well his behavior is fulfilling what he is trying to do. To be able to give feedback we need to identify something another person has done and let him know how we perceived it or how we felt about it. If he wants to, he can use that knowledge to check to see how well his behavior accomplished what he was intending to do.

There are some problems in receiving feedback.

1. One may get defensive, rejecting the information that was offered him, insisting, "That's not what I was doing at all."
2. One may listen only to what is favorable; if four persons said he talked too much and one person said he did not talk too much, he may prefer to listen to the latter.

There are also some problems in giving feedback.

We need to know how and when to offer it. Some suggestions are:

Speak to data—when specifically did you see and/or hear? Make it descriptive rather than judgmental. The statement "you talk too much" is one kind of feedback. "You spoke five times in the last ten minutes while several others who wanted to speak have not been able to" is a more helpful kind.

Give it at a useful level—speak to some behavior about which he can do something.

Give it as near to the time of action as possible.

Offer it rather than impose.

Check with others—"this is what I saw happening, is this the way you saw it?" This will confirm your observation of it and if you were not accurate in your perception, it can help to sharpen your sensitivity.

When there is the giving and receiving of feedback, certain things can happen.

Leveling—Telling another frankly about yourself, how you feel, what you are doing.

Confronting—Telling another how you feel with reference to his behavior.

Encounter and real *dialogue* can then follow.

JOHARI WINDOW

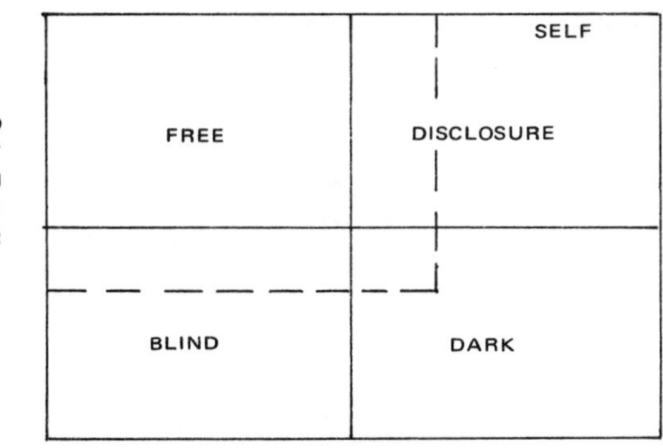

Another way of looking at the helpfulness of feedback is through what is called the Johari Window. This diagram represents the Self. The area marked "Free" is known to self and known to other, this is the area of mutual sharing and interaction: the area marked "Disclosure" is the hidden area, known to the self but unknown to others. It may remain thus hidden from others, yet some disclosure may also clear the air and aid relationships. The "Blind" area is unknown to self but known to others; this might include such features as the tone of one's voice, the expression on one's face, good traits of which we are unaware. The "Dark" area is unknown to self and unknown to others. This may include talents and abilities which are a part of your being but are at present inaccessible to you and unknown to others as well.

The dotted lines suggest the possibility of the solid line changing position. Openness or self-disclosure can reduce the hidden area and open up more of oneself to change or learning. However, whether or not to open this area is the individual's choice. Others have no right to invade.

Feedback can help to open up the "Blind" area of life. It can increase our self-awareness; to refer to our purpose, feedback can "help us to become aware of ourselves . . . as persons." The "Dark" area of life becomes available to us in moments of revelation, as the interaction of leveling and confronting brings insight to us and to others.

Moving Toward Confrontation

As we talk together in our group, we become aware of two levels of communication—content and process. The first, content, is the actual words being used. However, we don't any of us hear just words, but more particularly we "listen" to what goes with the words. We listen to inflections, volume, and other tonal qualities—to smiles or flushed faces, to all the subtle or obvious nonverbal messages sent our way by others which tend in fact, to outweigh the actual words in meaning. You might ask me, for example, a simple "How are you?" My verbal reply, "I'm just fine" could mean a dozen different things to you, ranging from "I couldn't be better!" to "I'm so-so" to "I'd rather not talk to you about it just now," depending on the *process* of verbalization. Process is what we need especially to identify and speak to each other about. *Process is real feeling life being demonstrated. The feelings are the facts!* Process, the real language of relationships, is a two-way street, in which chuckholes (made by circumstances over which there was no control) and self-made barriers to protect against unwanted or threatening traffic present blocks to easy interchange. Process may also be described as elusive, like the current of a stream. It's real. It's there, but if one scoops up a handful to examine it more closely, it disappears. Even as two people stop a conversation to discuss the process going on between them, the process changes! No one can claim perfect perception here, of course, but through training ourselves we can greatly improve our abilities to make more accurate guesses and thus measurably improve our communication with each other.

As you counsel the alcoholic, you may say phrases you feel are intended to be helpful, but the following might well happen:

Content	*Process*
I'm not certain I can help you but let's do the best we can.	I'm really scared of you but I know I'm supposed to help you.
What really seems to be your problem?	You've been lying up to now and I want the real truth.
Don't you realize that your wife is distraught over your actions?	You're a no-good insensitive slob who doesn't appreciate his wife.
You know you aren't unique in these feelings of guilt.	Why are you so full of self-pity?
I sure know how you feel.	Everybody has problems as great as yours.

If the language of relationship is of such importance in dealing with the alcoholic, then we need to consider the probable framework in which the counselor and alcoholic must begin a relationship. The following suggested framework holds within it the possibility of health and conversation or conversion for the alcoholic—or collusion between counselor and alcoholic, which neither wants but which both fear to uncover.

We are aware of the fact that the alcoholic has high defenses which are necessary for him to live with his compulsive behavior. The self-delusion and the defenses protect his sickness from identification. This means that so often when the counselor simply asks the alcoholic about "his drinking problem" he finds a great wall of denial. For the alcoholic doesn't "know" he is ill.

Final Syndetic Session Summarized

As each of us listed his learnings and new insights into himself (or "new" looks at old insights), a variety of defense mechanisms were also reported. Generally speaking, it was agreed that such defenses were largely unconscious and unnoticed until they had been confronted by the group experience.

There seemed also to be the realization by each of us that "living with our feelings" was a need we shared in common—that to do so is to live in the "here and now," and that this enables us to come to know ourselves and others as persons rather than "images."

A number of us described how acceptance of alcoholism as an illness was for us not an intellectual problem but rather an emotional block.

There was general agreement that both compulsive behavior and self-delusion were real. We had seen them present in ourselves or others in the group.

Our final session (which was a kind of Step Four) found us honestly trying to evaluate our present condition. The question being faced was, "Who am I?" Our verbal descriptions followed (and were a form of Step Five—"We admitted to ourselves, to God, and to other human beings the exact nature of our wrongs"), and we felt a number of reactions apparent at this point. The following are some of them.

What Learnings About Yourself Can You List and Describe?

I learned that my inadequacy is not as much of a detriment to me as I had thought.

Being able to accept getting backed into a corner and recognizing when I am backed into a corner, I am now able to try to control my defense mechanisms. I do not feel the frustration that I did feel from walking away from a situation, but rather a feeling of deep warmth and satisfaction that I can recognize and accept my inadequacies.

Confrontation from surrounding people who are human beings like myself does have a meaningful purpose, not to destroy one or his image, but rather to build confidence and new strength within the person being confronted.

I also learned that being conning or cunning can be harmful, not only to other people, but to myself, and it hurts.

I learned how much of a con artist I really am. I did believe this was true of me when I was a practicing alcoholic, but I was not aware of this now. I can truly see how I have sucked people into liking me by how I use this story of my family situation. They pity me or feel sorry for me and I use my physical handicap to bring on this pity.

I learned that I can get so scared and my anxiety level get so high that I couldn't hear the words of people who were talking directly to me. My mind was such a blank that I was not able to hear Bob say something that was funny. I didn't even hear the words, but the worst part of the whole thing is the con—when everyone else laughed, so did I, and not knowing what I was laughing about.

I recognize the "good guy" role as a cover-up for my gross inadequacy. This defense has worked so well over the years that I had myself convinced.

I learned of my protective defenses, and I did not realize it showed so much. This was proven to me when I literally reached out to protect Dick.

I learned that this quirk of mine about "Red" is an obsession. I've got to remember that other things are much more important; time should not be wasted dwelling on this.

As a result of these discoveries, I feel much closer to my "roomie" Irene. The rest of the group are much closer to me. This group was, and is, and will be an inspiration for me.

I have learned that my feelings are more accurate than communicating orally.

I have become aware of all my feelings as they each are. My feelings of fear, anger, pity, concern, sad, happy, good, mad, anxiety, hostility were recognized through the group.

When caught unaware by a threat, I clam up as a defense. This was brought home to me in vivid fashion when role-playing, when the counselor attacked me for suggesting that I, the patient, was ready to go home. My anxiety rose to such a level that I was incapable of assessing the situation. Had I recognized the fear, I would have handled it.

I am becoming more adept at recognizing my defenses now that I'm aware of what they are.

I have come to realize that up to this time I was always inclined to project to myself that I was someone I am not. I came to realize I was a real phony in ways. One was that I did admit I was an alcoholic, but I was not as bad as other alcoholics.

I thought that when I did something, I should be noticed. I felt that the group was leaving me out. When Blanche became angry and said her feelings, I realized that this was me. I shut the group out, but finally began to feel the concern they had for me.

I am aware that my character defects are me and always will be me.

I am able to accept myself as a person with all of my character defects. Learned that my self-evaluation was very low.

I learned that I have deep guilts which I never forgave myself for, which I see now kept me very defensive.

I did not know that I was hostile.

Self-Delusion

I believe that one can almost make himself believe in his anxieties, and I sincerely believe that this is self-delusion.

You can say that again! I've been telling myself what I am not for a long time.

Delusions to me are made with defense mechanisms. The delusions are seen by other people more than myself. A few of mine are the conning and manipulation and joking and laughing which I think tie in with delusion.

Self-delusion is seeing myself as something other than I am. This is easy to do if my defenses prevent me from seeing the real me. When my feelings are not acknowledged, I cannot see myself as I am; I see only what I want to see.

Self-delusion is easy to see in the alcoholic. He says things such as: "I do not drink in the morning, I do not miss work, etc." Persons who have attained some sobriety may start to think that they can start drinking again and become social drinkers.

Compulsive Behavior

Compulsive behavior can be learned by continuous practice of a behavioral pattern.

Compulsive behavior can be due to a confronting situation which annoys us before we stop and think.

It is recognized through inadequacies that are projected by another person to you and pose a threat to your ego or to the state of self-protection which you have readily employed within yourself.

Yes, I find myself wanting to be in the front seat or to speak all the time. When it gets down to the nitty-gritty, I pull in my horns and let someone else take the play, and I come out on safe ground.

I feel at times that there are things which we are compelled to do. We let our compulsion lead us, which could be a disastrous thing.

It is a quick reaction, such as is used as defense mechanism. It could also be made useful in counseling.

Compulsive behavior is a blind reaction to a stimulus, probably learned by frequent repetition.

When caught unaware by a threat, I run. This is my unreasoned response. When I am aware of this emotion I can accept it, and my behavior is no longer dictated by it. I am my own master again.

Compulsive behavior is people who drink to excess time after time. They come to believe and assume that if they take a couple of drinks first thing in the morning, that they will be OK for the day.

Compulsive behavior is my way, you *better* listen to me.

Fixing and Here and Now Data

Fixing is a means of escape from reality.

There is no way anyone can fix the disease of alcoholism.

"You want me to fix you, don't you?" was said to me in the group. God knows I wish you would have, but now I realize you couldn't. Make me feel good, yes, but not solve my problems. It was explained to me that I would have been a good advice-giver. I found myself thinking: "If I were you, I would do it this way, etc."

Fixing is "apple-polishing." This is a cover-up and could be a very dangerous area.

Why worry about there and then? Get those feelings out and dwell more on the here and how. This is a big hang-up with me.

Fixing is the switch the patient wants the counselor to turn on or off.

There and then data is data from outside the group. Here and now is data that is happening in this group setting at the present time.

I understand fixing is doing for the patient as opposed to letting him do it himself. This is akin to the parent doing his child's homework.

You might compare there and then vs. here and now data to the family finances. The money I have to live on is real and usable, what I've spent is gone, and next week's income isn't here yet. My feelings now are the only real me.

Fixing is telling the patient his feelings instead of trying to help him realize his own feelings.

He needs to be confronted with present-time data. Yesterday is not really important. Here and now problems at hand are what we should be concerned with.

Fixing as I understand it, was to express my feelings within to the other person that I felt he had.

Is Alcoholism a Disease?

Yes, because one's addiction to chemicals is uncontrollable and unpredicted. Alcoholism is an illness that one does not go out to look for or buy. It just happens.

One frustrating thing is that alcoholism cannot be cured. It affects many parts of the body. It is also an emotional illness. It can be controlled with insight and understanding.

The effects on the human body sometimes are readily visible and at other times have to be probed for by another person.

Yes, going back to my own experience, I can see how my own behavior was. Early in my life as I look back I became preoccupied with alcohol, not realizing it till the last.

Alcoholism is an incurable illness.

Alcoholism is a progressive illness. Alcohol is a chemical and it is a depressant. In the beginning it takes us into a realm of euphoria, but the illness keeps demanding more consumption of the chemical. We go back into a world of fear, and the only way out is to drink again. Alcoholism is hard to accept by the victim.

Anyone dependent on a chemical for functioning is not being himself. He is ill.

It is an illness that cannot be cured, but with proper treatment and follow-up can be arrested.

Alcoholism is a disease, but alcohol is not the problem, we are. The alcoholic is a person who is dependent upon chemical alcohol in order to function. It is not wanting to face reality.

Appendix I

CLERGYMAN'S HANDBOOK

AN INTRODUCTION TO STEPS IV, V, AND VI

Took a Fearless and Searching Moral Inventory of Ourselves

An Introduction to Step Four

Having passed at long last through the baffling barrier of denial of the existence of the illness, the alcoholic reaches the point where the admissions contained in Step One can be made in some kind of meaningful fashion. He is powerless, and his life is unmanageable. In this thoroughly depressed and hopeless condition, he finds it necessary (and in a measure possible) to accept a growing institution that while he has proven that he is utterly incapable of helping himself, there is restoration to be found with a Higher Power (Step Two). He has, at depth, entered the process of surrender which is the central psychological and spiritual factor of the recovery program. He continues this process by making the decision to turn his will, now recognized as unreliable, and his life, whatever it is or is not worth, over to the care of God as he at that moment "understands Him" (Step Three).

Here it would appear that many times the alcoholic, feeling as completely estranged from God as he does, tends to bog down in vain attempts at "understanding Him." Here he needs to be reminded that God by definition is beyond man's comprehension and that His ways are inscrutable, and to be turned rather to the other person named in the step. He himself has become such a person as he cannot now recognize. He realizes at this point that quite literally he is a stranger to himself and that here greater knowledge and understanding *can* be achieved and indeed must *first be* achieved. In other words, if this decision is to be carried through at any significant level existentially, the alcoholic has to come to know who is that self he wants to surrender; his basic need is for greater self-awareness. (Such self-awareness, he has yet to discover, will tend in fact to reveal what his beliefs concerning God are.)

The technique for developing his ability to rediscover himself is a personal moral inventory wherein the characteristics behind his moral anxiety and guilt are examined as fearlessly and as forthrightly as possible, so that this burden may be reduced to manageable levels.

Here the aim is to help him to see that his past behavior is what he has to identify with, and to begin his acceptance of that identification. More than that, however, the goal is for him to see his behavior as a revelation of his character. These were the specific defeats of character which resulted in the behavior pattern about which he feels guilty (i.e., he did that particular thing *because* he was proud, or resentful, or sensitive, etc.).

Here, too, care is exercised to help him avoid unnecessary preoccupation with the question of why he became an alcoholic, which remains essentially a mystery. Rather, he is helped to see the continuance of these defects as *obstructions* to his recovery from the illness.

Moreover, since his condition is one of ambivalence, the aim is to assist him in discovering the conflicts of character that exist within him. (I'm not a person, I'm a civil war!) It is not that he is completely devoid of values, but rather it is likely that his is a "high" value system, with which his behavior has in fact been at odds. His conscience has been and is speaking to real guilt, and that guilt must now be faced with as little evasion as possible (Step Five).

At the same time, his ambivalence should also be explored in the direction of the positive attributes of character present in the individual. Often this can be done quite effectively simply by reexamining some of the defects themselves. For example, the sensitivity which led to self-pity and concomitant destructive behavior may also be used in being sensible to and sympathetic with the problems and joys of others and corresponding positive behavior. Similarly guilt is generally regarded as a negative condition, and yet guilt *examined* will reveal the nature and reality of his value system, the very existence of which he has been doubting, etc.

Also, it would seem that within this inventory the individual should be guided in the thorough exploration of his identification with the illness concept; not in order to make use of it to "get off the hook" of guilt and anxiety, but to move in the direction of removing all equivocation characterologically. Thus, in facing the truth about himself, he might sum it up: "This then *is* I, God help me!" or "I *am* sick, and not only physically, but mentally and spiritually!" At the same time, he is recognizing such positive attributes as may be present, and growing in the intuition that, with the help of God, the negative conditions may be changed and these positive elements built upon as he moves toward a relatively normal and healthy life.

Admitted to God, to ourselves, and to Another Human Being the Exact nature of Our Wrongs.

An Introduction to Step Five

The alcoholic has now become reacquainted with himself at some kind of more meaningful level. Next he bolsters his decision to turn himself over to God, as he now understands Him, by revealing himself to Him. His self-awareness is "hammered home" by an act of self-revelation to God and another human being. He admits "the exact nature of his wrongs."

The effect of this new degree of self-awareness has been to create the need for a reduction of the burden of moral anxiety and guilt which it has brought into conscious focus. Communication at a level of such depth as *actually to reduce* these unwanted symptoms is the suggested procedure.

Here it would seem that most alcoholics require assistance in the recognition of their need so to communicate, as the most effective way to deal with this burden, as well as how to do so. Often their very defects (pride, self-pity, rationalization, etc.), joined with some or many of the personality traits of the anxious person (weak ego, timidity, etc.), make successful communication a most difficult endeavor. Moreover, since their lives have been conditioned for more or less long periods of time to a growing separation from other persons, their ability to relate verbally to another person has suffered from disuse and needs relearning. They need help in the acceptance of the truth that such "meaningful communication" is the mark of "normal living"—those who achieve and maintain mental and spiritual health continually engage themselves in such communication.

Here, they should be cautioned, it would seem that real care should be exercised concerning the person with whom the Fifth Step is made. Such a person should be one who is thoroughly acquainted with the Twelve Steps and an experienced counselor. Some members of the clergy seem best to fit these qualifications, for the most part. When clergy are so used, it should be clearly understood by both listener and alcoholic that the aim of this admission is not absolution in the sacramental sense (though this may rightly be encouraged for the proper persons at that or another time) but rather a frank revelation of the character of the alcoholic. In other words, the purpose is not simply to list a long series of wrong actions or to review a pattern of shameful behavior; though this will undoubtedly happen as either preface or proof, but to reveal the exact *nature* of the person who did these things. The behavior is in the past tense, but the defects are present and persistent. Here the alcoholic needs guidance both in advance of the step and during it, lest he allow himself, or be allowed by the listener, to continue to evade his confrontation of himself through such forms of communication as can, however insidiously, deny, or rationalize, or project his real character conflicts.

If the listener is experienced enough and aware enough of the goals involved, he will be quick to point out such attempts when they occur. When sentences begin with "When I was drinking, I" or "Perhaps it was true, I" or "Though it wasn't often, I"; "Whenever my wife was angry, I" or "Though it didn't hurt the children really, I," the listener will stop the speaker promptly and call attention to what is happening. The goal is to have the alcoholic speak of himself directly and unequivocally. Thus he might summarize with some such thought as, "I *did* those things because I *am* this kind of person, God help me!" (Here perhaps it should be pointed out to the listener that he must allow the speaker to *experience the pain* he is attempting to describe. This is not the time to reassure or minimize, but rather to draw out what has so long been hidden. What the speaker experiences rather than what the listener says is the therapeutic agent involved.)

In some fashion, the alcoholic begins now to see the truth that these defects of character are the signs of his sickness and that upon their removal his recovery depends. Here, as the process of surrender continues, the next need is created and experienced (Step Six). He will need to *become willing* to have them removed.

Somewhere around this stage of his progress, he will now have to face and come to grips with the whole complicated and necessary process of forgiveness as it relates to himself and his divine and human relationships. The alcoholic seems to approach this process with more difficulty than most; undoubtedly because of the unusually depressed state of his self-esteem. The dynamics intrinsic to divine forgiveness, self-forgiveness, and interpersonal forgiveness need thorough review, since they seem basic to this and the other steps through Nine.

Some Spiritual Dynamics of Forgiveness

I. Forgiveness is a corporate process, requiring at least two persons, since it is based on relationship. Its goal is to restore broken relationships at a level enhancing to the lives of both persons involved as individuals.

A. A destructive action or negative attitude from one person toward another will tend to weaken or destroy whatever mutual relationship has existed up to that point.

B. Generally speaking, only a process involving some form of inward admission of fault, real remorse, outward expression of guilt, and earnest desire for proper restitution which is acceptable to the injured person (and then actually accepted) can restore relationship.

C. Forgiveness leads to a mutual acceptance by each individual of the other as he is, and implies restored trust and good will.

II. Restored relationship is costly to *both* individuals involved.

A. Both must have a value system known to themselves and recognized by each other.

B. The person whose act or behavior was the immediate cause of the break in relationship is to admit culpability, feel remorse, and act in the direction of communicating guilt and seeking restitution at whatever cost in pride or self-esteem. Basically, his problem is to identify himself with the original destructive action, the destructive results of the action, and the need to initiate restoration.

C. The injured person is to accept the attempts at reconciliation by paying the price of his own pride, self-image, self-pity, etc. Often this is more difficult because he does not see himself as in any way responsible, much less culpable. (To be unable to forgive is a condition involving not only rigidity but many negative and destructive factors very difficult to recognize and accept—i.e., self-pity, self-righteousness, envy, etc.) Basically, his problem is to identify with the other person at such depth as will recognize that person's behavior as one that can bring remorse and this time *does*, and to accept destructive human behavior in general as something of which he himself is not only capable but often guilty.

III. The payment of these costs results not only in restored relationship but in strengthened (or matured) individual lives.

A. The effect of admitting culpability, feeling actual remorse, and then entering into restorative action is to strengthen the weakened ego of the injurer. He "feels better," which is to say that he is more self-accepting. He is more in a position where he can "forgive himself." His character conflicts can more easily be reduced. He is, therefore, better able to forgive someone else.

B. In his identification with the behavior of the other person, as well as with that person, much the same positive consequence ensues for the injured person. He too "feels better," is more self-accepting, and achieves some reduction of his own character conflicts. In forgiving another he is "forgiving himself" as well.

IV. Over-all, the experience of human forgiveness by either the injurer or the injured has a deeper benefit spiritually. This increased understanding of what is a desirable sense of well-being at the human level has the effect of opening the door to the reception of divine forgiveness.

A. The blocks or obstructions to divine human relationships are very often guilt-centered. Estrangement from God is not caused simply by a scrupulous wrathful or righteous "God image," but by the self-loathing and self-condemnation of the guilt-ridden individual.

B. Reduction of the guilt and moral anxiety allows greater fredom to accept the intuitive insight that God's love and mercy are real and available. ("If ye, being evil, know how to give good gifts unto your children, how much more will the Heavenly Father give the Holy Spirit to them who ask Him?" Luke 11:13)

C. Acceptance of divine forgiveness becomes an "enabling" dynamic in maintaining current and future human relationships whenever they tend toward strain or disruption. ("For if you forgive men their trespasses, your Heavenly Father will also forgive you." Matt. 6:14)

V. The actual experience of divine, self-, and interpersonal forgiveness, over a period of time and more or less consistently, tends to provide a climate for "spiritual growth and health."

A. Such attitudes as resentment, pride, self-pity, etc. are more readily recognized as destructive and more directly dealt with as needing removal.

B. Such attitudes as faith, care, or concern for others, love, compassion, etc. are seen as not only possible but desirable, and are therefore sought out and consciously nurtured.

VI. Restored relationship is essential to the securing and maintaining of meaningful and satisfying living for the individual.

A. The essential loneliness of both the unforgiven and the unforgiving is experienced as the hell it describes, and leads to the "sickness unto death."

B. Restoration is experienced as positive emotion and attitude, love, gratitude, joy, etc., which are seen as synonymous with "life." (Cf. Parable of Prodigal Son, Luke 15:11—end: "Bring the fatted calf; let us eat and make merry for this my Son was dead and is alive again!")

Were Entirely Ready to Have God Remove All These Defects of Character

An Introduction to Step Six.

Having dealt with his moral anxiety and guilt in this direct fashion (Step Five), which did have the effect of reducing the long-borne burden, the alcoholic now is better able to view himself critically in an even more dispassionate and constructive way. He sees himself as one whose previous life and specific behavior have resulted from certain definite character conflicts. At this point, he can not only recognize and name many of these conflicts, but he has identified with them. They are his. He can describe himself and his condition—and that pretty accurately. Yet it is not enough. He needs now to be assisted in realizing that he has come only partially into the surrender process that can result in his recovery. His defenses, so elaborately erected over the years, have been destroyed. Self-delusion has been replaced by admission of his condition, and in some real sense acceptance of it. He is capable even of seeing that what he passed off as acceptance in the past was, in truth, simply compliance. Now however he needs help to see that his condition not only *was* one of compliance, but that there is that within him which is fighting to keep it so. If this current condition persists, his recovery will be more than handicapped. It is one thing to "accept" at a conscious intellectual level and quite another to do so at the unconsious, emotional, characterological, or "gut" level as well. The fuller meaning of becoming *entirely* ready, not only to see the wisdom of a change, but the absolute necessity for it, becomes apparent. Being entirely ready implies being ready with the entire or total being, conscious and unconscious, and not simply "thoroughly" ready. Once again he is faced by the question of the depth of his identification with the illness concept. If he is to recover, this basic conflict must be resolved. He is sick. He can get well. Accomplishing this involves his becoming *entirely ready to change.* The battle of the ego has yet to be won.

As Dr. Harry M. Tiebout puts it, "The capacity of the Ego to bypass experience is astounding and would be humorous were it not so tragic in its consequences. Cutting the individual down to size and making the results last is a task never completely accomplished. The possibility of a return of his Ego must be faced by every alcoholic. If it does return, he may refrain from drinking but he will surely go on a 'dry drunk,' with all the old feelings and attitudes once more asserting themselves and making sobriety a shambles of discontent and restlessness. Not until the Ego is decisively retired can peace and quiet again prevail. As one sees this struggle in process, the need for the helping hand of a Deity becomes clearer. Mere man alone all too often seems powerless to stay the force of his Ego. He needs outside assistance and needs it urgently" *(The Ego Factors in Surrender in Alcoholism,* p. 620—see Reading List, p. 117 of this volume.)

In some way, then, not yet well explained, the depth of his motivations are related to the quality of the surrender he now, hopefully, experiences. His cry is, "Oh, that a man might arise in me that the man that I am would cease to be!" or "I don't know exactly what, but I'll do *anything* to change," or "If I don't change, I'm a dead man!"

Now he deepens the intuition of Step Two, where he came to believe in a Power able to restore him to sanity, as well as the decision of Step Three, where he decided to turn will and life over to God as he understood Him. Yet, ready though he may be, in point of fact the power to change is to be found outside himself. With this acknowledged need and the sense of his own inadequacy to meet it alone, he turns to Step Seven and humbly asks Him to remove all these defects of character. He enters into the final stages of the surrender process because he is *willing* to have these negative characteristics and attitudes removed, as well as actively to cooperate in the building upon his constructive attributes.